Collecte

Volume ꜰ ꜱꜱ ꞇ ᴦy

C000256564

Nigel Pearce

chipmunkapublishing
the mental health publisher

Published by
Chipmunkapublishing
United Kingdom

http://www.chipmunkapublishing.com

On the nature of poetics, my authorial development, and influences over the Master of Arts in Creative Writing. A study in dialectics.

There is no money in poetry, but there is no poetry in money either.
                              - Robert Graves. (attributed).

I would suggest that Robert Graves made a pertinent comment but lacked the methodology for understanding the nature of aesthetics. Thus, an appraisal of the creative processes involved in my authorial development over the M.A. in Creative Writing requires something rather more complex. The obvious question is, what is art and, more significantly, poetry? How does this mould my, indeed, anyone's artistic production, and how can this change over time? Once I have asked this question and answered it, I will be able to appraise my poetics in the light of the sources of my dissertation and my poetics in these contexts. I will seek a methodology, principally but not exclusively, in the writings of Karl Marx, Frederick Engels, Leon Trotsky, György Lukács and the recent research of John Molyneux (Molyneux, John (2020) The Dialectics of Art, Haymarket Books, Kindle Edition). I will argue that a gulf exists between how bourgeois and Marxist literary criticism understand poetics. However, this has its foundations in a profound difference in Weltanschauung or worldview and that this 'in the last instance' is determined by the socio-economic relations of an epoch. However, they cannot be reduced to these because Marxism and Marxist aesthetics are more complex than any reductive model.

I will also understand that William Wordsworth: (1802) Preface to Lyrical Ballads https://www.poetryfoundation.org/articles/69383/observations-prefixed-to-lyrical-ballads in which he argued for employing 'the language of ordinary men' and The Prelude (1805) made the introspective turn were highly significant. He was writing in the shadow of John Milton (1667/1674), Paradise Lost. Nevertheless, William Wordsworth created the foundation for what was to follow in Anglophone verse. In a new poetic revolution, Ezra Pound urged poets at the beginning of the next century to use these

Methods of writing in Retrospect (1918):
1) Direct treatment of the 'thing' whether subjective or objective 2) To use absolutely no word that did not contribute to the presentation 3) As regarding rhythm: to compose in sequence of the musical phrase, not in sequence of a metronome.
"A Retrospect" and "A Few Don'ts" by Ezra Pound | Poetry Foundation
Here is possibly the best-known poem in which the young Ezra Pound implemented his manifesto before his ideological degeneration into fascism:
In a Station on the Metro
The apparition of these faces in the crowd:
Petals on a wet, black bough.

— Poetry (April 1913)In a Station of the Metro by Ezra Pound | Poetry Magazine

Although William Carlos Williams (1968) The Autobiography of William Carlos Williams wrote that he was profoundly influenced by the young Ezra Pound yet:

I could never take him as a steady diet...What I could never tolerate in Pound or seek in myself was all his posturings as the poet.

-        William Carlos Williams (1968) The Autobiography of William Carlos Williams, USA MacGibbon & Kee Ltd p.58.

Of course, T.S. Eliot and Ezra Pound were pioneers of Modernism but William Carlos Williams' reaction to them was also significant for my poetry. He like William Wordsworth in England and Walt Whitman in America, embraced the language of the masses, the everyday. Here he, correctly in my view, argued regarding T.S. Eliot (1922) The Waste Land:

These were the years before the great catastrophe to our Letters-the appearance of The Waste Land...Our work staggered to a halt for a moment under the blast of Eliot's genius which gave the poem back to the academics. We did not know how to answer him. William Carlos Williams (1968) The Autobiography of William Carlos Williams, USA MacGibbon & Kee Ltd, p 146.

However, I shall also illustrate my development with Allen Ginsburg and James Wright's poetry to elucidate both my authorial choices and development.

.   Returning to the methodology for a framework in which to position my poetry. Marx did not leave a systematic aesthetic; however, Marx was deeply influenced by both poetry and literature . In his youth and young adulthood, Marx wrote poetry . His enduring friendship with Heinrich Heine is illustrative of this characteristic of Karl Marx's thinking and personality. However, where do we begin without a systematic
 poetic? The response is straightforward and is derived from György Lukács' (1921) History and Class Consciousness: Studies in Marxist Dialectics:

Let us assume for the sake of argument that recent research had disproved once and for all every one of Marx's individual theses. Even if this were to be proved, every serious 'orthodox' Marxist would still be able to accept all such modern findings without reservation and hence dismiss all of Marx's theses in toto – without having to renounce his orthodoxy for a single moment. Orthodox Marxism, therefore, does not imply the uncritical acceptance of the results of Marx's investigations. It is not the 'belief' in this or that thesis, nor the exegesis of a 'sacred' book. On the contrary, orthodoxy refers exclusively to method.
   -
https://www.marxists.org/archive/lukacs/works/history

Thus, Marxist analysis has a method that is fundamental to its nature for György Lukács and that was Historical Materialism. Therefore, he had questioned Frederick Engels's position on the scientific validity of Dialectical Materialism. This is a fascinating controversy within Marxism, but I do not have the space to articulate it with any justice. I will only say I accept much of György Lukács' earlier work but also agree with the general direction of Engel's investigations and codifications of Dialectical Materialism (Marx did not use the phrase), and Engel's positions, mainly in the later letters, bolster my argument for writing a Marxian poetic. However, György Lukács' (1921) History of Class Consciousness and its emphasis 'on method', although vital, does not nullify the reality that Marx's and other's material texts are significant for both the poet and critic. Here we see Marx writing lyrically about Milton's Paradise Lost in this relatively late text of 1862 & 1863:

Milton produced Paradise Lost in the way that a silkworm produces silk as the expression of his own Nature.

- Marx, Karl, Theories of Surplus Value, Moscow, Progress Publishers, 1963, p. 401.

This does not seem to resonate immediately with either Historical or Dialectical Materialism, but as John Molyneux (2020) argued cogently:

Of course, this is a somewhat inaccurate way of describing the writing of poetry; however, he clearly means by this that it was labour in which Milton affirmed and expressed himself (i.e., unalienated labour), and he insists that the character of this labour is not changed by the subsequent fact that the product is sold as a commodity. The second distinction is between Milton (the artist) and the 'literary proletarian' who 'delivers hackwork' on the orders of a publisher. In practice, these distinctions may not be simple or absolute, with intermediate cases where the pressures of the market react back on the writer or artist without totally controlling their work, as is the case with normal wage labour. Nevertheless, they point to features that are typical of the situation of the artist under capitalism.

-        Molyneux, John (2020) The Dialectics of Art, p 43.

Here we can perceive an innovative Marxist aesthetic. I shall delineate the origins and conclusions of John Molyneux's (2020), Dialectics of Art. His first steppingstone in developing a new Marxian poetic was to reference Trotsky's often neglected contributions to the field of aesthetics:

Another important influence was Leon Trotsky. Trotsky's main influence on me was in terms of revolutionary theory, but his Literature and Revolution and his essays in Leon Trotsky on Literature and Art made a huge impression. I very much agreed with his vehement defence of artistic freedom…and his insistence that art should be judged according to the 'law of art'. However, I don't think Trotsky, who had rather a lot of other things on his plate, ever really explained what the 'law of art' was. Anyway, it got me thinking, and some of the results can be seen in this book.

-        Molyneux, John. (2020) The Dialectics of Art p. 11. Haymarket Books. Kindle Edition.

For Molyneux (2020), the question is, is artistic labour under capitalism 'alienated labour power' or 'non-alienated labour power'. This has significant ramifications for my poetics, concurrent creative processes, and authorial choices, as I will elaborate upon later. For Molyneux, artistic labour-power is not estranged from the poet or artist in the same manner that the majority of proletarians are alienated from their 'labour-power'. They are alienated from the product of their labour, from each other and from Nature. The proletarian's experience of capitalism is far greater than economic exploitation, as expressed in Marx's Labour Theory of Value. But here, we have the foundation for the Marxian understanding of creativity. As Marx so well encapsulated it as early in his maturation as 1844:

The entire so-called history of the world is nothing but the creation of man through human labour.
- Karl Marx, Economic and Philosophic Manuscripts of 1844, Moscow: Progress Publishers, 1967, p. 106.

Therefore, for Marx, human labour holds the potential for creativity.

However, Molyneux (2020) intriguingly moved beyond his reinterpretation of the Classical Marxist opus and connected an analysis of Form and Content to revisiting that. The innovation in György Lukács' (1921) History of Class Consciousness made this reassessment legitimate for Marxian socialists, i.e., texts are not hammered into laws of stone because, as with the dialectic, there is always motion in History. John Molyneux (2020) wrote:

The fact that art is non-alienated labour cannot be the end of the story because there is a great deal of unalienated labour that is not and does not produce art.

- Molyneux, John. (2020) p. 38. Haymarket Books. Kindle Edition.

So how can we define when unalienated labour is art and when it is not. Molyneux provided an explanation:

The answer lies in the nature of the relationship between form and content that prevails in these categories, as opposed to the relationship that obtains in art. In a work of scientific or social theory, the content is not only much more important than the form, but it is also, to a large extent, detachable from it. In a work of art the content/meaning is totally bound up with the form and is inseparable from it.… And by 'form', I do not mean genre or formal structure, as in a poem that is a sonnet or in rhyming couplets, or in a watercolour painting, or in music, a blues piece, or a concerto. I mean the concrete form of a particular work: in the case of a poem, every single word in that exact order.

-        Molyneux, John (2020) p. 39. Haymarket Books. Kindle Edition.

John Molyneux concluded his position with a sense of satisfaction, which is appropriate in my opinion because this is an advance in Marxian, indeed all aesthetics:

To conclude, art is work produced by unalienated human labour and characterised by a fusion or unity of form and content. Furthermore, there is a connection between these two elements in the definition in that, generally speaking, it requires unalienated labour to achieve such a fusion of form and content.... To the best of my knowledge, the precise definition of art presented here has not been advanced previously,

- Molyneux, John (2020) p. 42.
Haymarket Books. Kindle Edition.

I have illustrated this argument freely with quotations from John Molyneux's recent book for three reasons. Firstly, I am persuaded that it is a significant contribution to Marxist aesthetics; secondly, it has created much debate on the Left, both of which are noteworthy and to be applauded and finally, because Molyneux (2020) constructs a framework for understanding my poetry and poetics.

Nevertheless, the position of the writer under capitalism is one of estrangement even if her or his 'labour-power' is not alienated. We may be in control of our labour power, but the poet is surely a pariah in the world as it is presently constituted. We live with authenticity in a world defined by Jean-Paul Sartre's 'bad faith.' For the poet must as Simone Weil suggested: 'Refuse to be an accomplice. Don't lie-don't keep your eyes shut.' Simone Weil in (Zaretsky, Robert (2022) The Subversive Simone Weil: A Life in Five Ideas, Chicago, University of Chicago Press, p. 39). For example, Allen Ginsburg (1956) Howl:

Howl.

For Carl Solomon.

I saw the best minds of my generation destroyed
by madness, starving hysterical naked,
dragging themselves through the negro streets at
dawn looking for an angry fix,
angelheaded hipsters burning for the ancient
heavenly connection to the starry dynamo in the
machinery of night,
who poverty and tatters and hollow-eyed and high
sat up smoking in the supernatural darkness of
cold-water flats floating across the tops of cities
contemplating jazz, [...]
Howl by Allen Ginsberg | Poetry Foundation

This was a very influential poem regarding the
development of my poetic in my pre-F71
development and remains so and was reinforced
by the course materials in A803 in sections like
Experimental Approaches. This is an example
from the EMA in-progress:

In the Laboratory.

Red tentacles are gripping the wasted wail of a
seething brain which writhes in delirium with a
rush, white light

C H N10 15
Eyes hang loose, attached only by yellow threads
to grey sockets,
They melted a millisecond ago and now are
dripping,

Dropping by diamond drop into a culture dish, the
doctor makes a smear,
Places a slide beneath the lens of a microscope
and peers in,
A banshee screams into her eyes; she jumps back
too late,
The laboratory rotates into concentric circles; it
has become a phantasmagoria,
 That pain had gone; those chemical lights blazed,
but she lost a rational brain.

 Note: C H N10 15 is the formula for
methamphetamine (Methedrine).

I employed a variety of poetic techniques including
the insertion of a scientific formula inspired by the
use of allusion in the early writing of Marianne
Moore (2016) Observations. Also, I made
alliterative cuts with 'c' sounds in the penultimate
and final lines. I 'show' under the influence of Allen
Ginsberg (2001) and Elise Cowen (2014) the
relationship between altered states of
consciousness and poetry.
    Therefore, there is an apparent opposition
between the poet's objective position under
capitalism as possessing 'non-alienated labour
power' (Molyneux) and the lived experience. Lenin
illustrates how reality is in a condition of dialectical
opposition and this, I argue, applies to poets as
well:
        The condition for the knowledge of all
processes of the world…

in real life is the knowledge of them as opposites.
- V.I. Lenin. Lenin Collected Works: Volume 38: Philosophical Notebooks

Hence, we can understand the dialectical relationship between, firstly the objective and subjective roles of the poet and secondly, the contradictory experience of the poet and capitalism which is one of alienation. A conflict which can only be resolved, with a synthesis in a qualitatively different society, I suggest. I illustrate the latter with another poem from the EMA because the only authentic response to this experience is to resist, I argue. Although this poem is about a different epoch and having learnt the lessons of History, revolutionaries reject these tactics and, again, understand the class-conscious proletariat as the instrument of social transformation:

Lines on Brigitte M' a leading member of the S.P.K (Socialist Patients' Collective).

A chill and steel grimace glares and stares
From the steel goblet from which she sips,
Substitutions are easy in the class struggle,
She didn't substitute emotions with zeros.

Replace the proletariat with a vanguard?
Never replace authenticity with their shit,
Kill a revolutionist with a gun or tablets
Yet they will rise like your fear of death.

From this cup drunk Brigitte M, not the

China tea-services of the oppressor,
She smiled as that red wine of love
Intoxicated her with a fantastic desire

To destroy daddy in every manifestation.
She was an incarnation, the realisation,
And the red insurrection, of our revolution,
Her gun fired the lemon butterflies of love.

Note. The SPK were the 'second generation' of
the West German urban guerrilla group, the Red
Army Faction.
In this poem the inspiration for the disembodied
text, the quote from Sylvia Plath, was derived from
William Carlos Williams (2011) Spring and All and
Paterson in Collected Poems (2018/2019) vols 1 &
.2. The final stanza gains in strength from the
internal rhyme of the 'ion' sounds employing
assonance.

However, finally turning to the poetry of James
Wright, I note that I was only aware of him as the
first English translator of Hesse, Hermann (1970)
Poems until a series of emails with my tutor, which
opened a new world of a previously unknown
poet. The general critical view is that his poetry
reached a transformative moment with Wright
(1963) The Branch Will Not Break. However, I
prefer his (1959) Saint Judas which includes All
the Beautiful are Blameless with these final lines:
But the dead have no names,
they lie so still, And all the beautiful are blameless
now.

-       Wright, James, (1992) Above the River: The Collected Poems, New York, A Wesleyan University Press Edition., p.64.
Although this quotation from James Wright (1992 Above the Bridge: The Collected Poems) On a Phrase from Southern Ohio for Katherine Knight encapsulates much of the subjective undercurrent of my poetic:

And still in my dreams I sway like one fainting strand Of spider web, glittering and vanishing and frail Above the river.

- Wright, James (1992 Above the Bridge: The Collected Poems) p.301.

In conclusion, I agree with Karl Marx:

The revolution cannot take its poetry from the past, but only the future

.18th Brumaire of Louis Bonaparte. Karl Marx 1852 - Marxists

V. I. Lenin (1905) Lenin: Party Organisation and Party Literature - Marxists clarified what was a rather loose definition:

What is this principle of party literature? It is not simply that, for the socialist proletariat, literature cannot be a means of enriching individuals or groups: it cannot, in fact, be an individual undertaking, independent of the common cause of the proletariat.

Down with non-partisan writers! Down with literary supermen! Literature must become part of the common cause of the proletariat, "a cog and a screw" of one single great Social-Democratic mechanism set in motion by the entire politically-conscious vanguard of the entire working class.

- V.I. Lenin (1978) Lenin: On Art and Literature, Moscow,

Progress Publishers, p. 25.

And he continues with his finger on the pulse of History in the same 1905 article:

And we socialists expose this hypocrisy and rip off the false labels, not in order to arrive at a non-class literature and art (that will be possible only in a socialist extra-class society), but to contrast this hypocritically free literature, which is in reality linked to the bourgeoisie, with a really free one that will be openly linked to the proletariat. It will be a free literature because the idea of socialism and sympathy with the working people […].

- V.I. Lenin (1978) Lenin: On Art and Literature, Moscow,

Progress Publishers pp. 28-29.

Therefore, we must dare to write and dare to win. These are linked because it is only in a class freed of class antagonism that humanity can flourish for as Leon Trotsky (1924): 'The average human type will rise to the heights of an Aristotle, a Goethe, or a Marx. And above this ridge new peaks will rise.' https://www.marxists.org/archive/trotsky/1924/lit_r evo/

Finally, I argue, that another change in my authorial practice was derived from my tutor advising me to 'ground' my poetry and thus take the advice of The Imagists, 'there are no ideas but in things' as William Carlos Williams suggested in Paterson.

Bibliography.

Cowen, Elise (2014) Poems and Fragments, Ahsahta Press, Boise State University.

Di Prima, Diane (2011) Revolutionary Letters: Fiftieth Anniversary Edition, USA, Silver Press.

Eliot, T.S (1922) The Waste Land https://www.poetryfoundation.org/poems/47311/th e-waste-land

Ginsburg, Allen (1956) Howl, Howl by Allen Ginsberg | Poetry Foundation

Ginsberg, Allen (2001) Selected Poems 1947-1995, London, Penguin Modern Classics.

Hesse, Hermann (1970) [trans, Wright, James] Poems, New York, Farrar, Straus, and Giroux.

Lenin, V.I (1978) Lenin: On Art and Literature, Moscow, Progress Publishers.

Lenin, V.I Lenin: Party Organisation and Party Literature – Marxists

Lenin, V.I Lenin Collected Works: Volume 38: Philosophical Notebooks

Lukács, György (1921) History and Class Consciousness: Studies in Marxist Dialectics: https://www.marxists.org/archive/lukacs/works/hist ory

Marx, Karl (1967) Economic and Philosophic Manuscripts of 1844, Moscow: Progress Publishers.

Marx, Karl,.18th Brumaire of Louis Bonaparte. Karl Marx 1852 - Marxists

Marx, Karl (2013) Selected Poetry, India, LeoPard Books.

Marx, Karl, (1963) Theories of Surplus Value, Moscow, Progress Publishers.

Mew, Charlotte (2000) [ed] Newton, John Complete Poems, London, Penguin Classics.

Mew, Charlotte (2008) [ed] Boland, Eavan Selected Poems, Manchester, Carcanet Books.

Milton, John (2008), Milton: The Major Works, Oxford, Oxford World Classics.

Molyneux, John. (2020) Dialectics of Art, Haymarket Books. Kindle Edition.

Moore, Marianne (2016), Observations, New York, Farrer, Strauss, and Giroux.

Plath, Sylvia (2004) Ariel: The Restored Edition, London, Faber & Faber.

Pound, Ezra— Poetry (April 1913)In a Station of the Metro by Ezra Pound | Poetry Magazine

Pound, Ezra (1918)
"A Retrospect" and "A Few Don'ts" by Ezra Pound | Poetry Foundation

Prawer, S.S. (2011) Karl Marx and World Literature, London, Verso Books.

Sartre, Jean-Paul (1974) Existentialism and Humanism, London, Methuen Publishing Ltd

Smith, Dave (1982) The Pure Clear Word: Essays on the Poetry of James Wright. Chicago, University of Illinois Press.

Trotsky, Leon, (1992) Art and Revolution: Writings on Literature, Politics, and Culture by Leon Trotsky, New York, Pathfinder

Trotsky, Leon, (2009) Literature and Revolution, Chicago., Haymarket Books.
https://www.marxists.org/archive/trotsky/1924/lit_revo/

Weil, Simone in (Zaretsky, Robert (2022) The Subversive Simone Weil: A Life in Five Ideas. London, University of Chicago Press.

Williams, William Carlos (1968) The Autobiography of William Carlos Williams, USA MacGibbon & Kee Ltd.

Williams, William Carlos (2018) Collected Poems Volume I: 1909-1939. Manchester, Carcanet.

Williams, William Carlos (2019) Collected Poems Volume II: 1939-1962, Manchester, Carcanet.

Williams, William Carlos (2011) Spring and All, Facsimile Edition, New York, A New Directions Book.

Wordsworth, William (1802) Preface to Lyrical Ballads. https://www.poetryfoundation.org/articles/69383/observations-prefixed-to-lyrical-ballads

Wordsworth, William (1979) The Prelude 1799, 1805, 1850: Authoritative Texts, Context and Reception, Recent Critical Essays. New York, Norton Critical Editions.

Wright, James, (1992) Above the River: The Collected Poems, New York, A Wesleyan University Press Edition, Chicago, University of Chicago Press.

Wright, James (2005) Selected Poems, USA, Wesleyan University Press.

Hugh MacDiarmid the poetics of engagement and its methods:
On being 'myriad minded' in Three Hymns to Lenin.
Every door in any town should be wide open to that great lyric poet Hugh MacDiarmid, a light burning in every window, food and drink on each table, and a bed aired, with sheets. If only one could think of all the statues that will one day be put up to him all over Scotland, work out roughly how much these statues will cost and give him the money now. Posterity can look after itself: that is its function. Honour the brief lives now.

- Dylan Thomas,
 Hugh MacDiarmid: Second Hymn to Lenin (Spring 1960) (marxists.org)

I am forty-six; of tenacious, long-lived country folk.
Fools regret my poetic change--from my 'enchanting early lyrics.
But I have found in Marxism all that I need--
- Hugh MacDiarmid. Collected Poems (1978) Vol 1, p, 615.

One major shortcoming in my writing that concentrating on Three Hymns to Lenin (1957) may help to correct in my authorial practice is to 'focus' more and not 'be wildly subjective' as my tutor pointed out in my last script. Writing with 'focus' is not always easy when writing through the prism of MH issues. However, hopefully, my study of this collection may help correct this problem. Although MacDiarmid had a breakdown in 1935, he published Second Hymn to Lenin that year although it was written in 1932. MacDiarmid in Three Hymns to Lenin (1957) deals with complex and convoluted material but stays eminently 'focused.' This is one of the many lessons I hope to learn from Hugh MacDiarmid. I note that MacDiarmid drew on eclectic sources and would repeatedly utter this quote from Thomas Hardy as in MacDiarmid: a festschrift (1962) p,11: 'From the beginning, I took as my motto-and have adhered to it all through my literary life - 'Literature is the expression of revolt against accepted things.'

Hugh MacDiarmid worked in a factory supporting the struggle against fascism during World War Two. But as my tutor said his work was indeed wonderfully ambitious. He challenged the English Ascendancy in culture by writing in dialect and created the Scottish Renaissance. Two of his three hymns to Lenin were written in such dense dialect that I had to use a Scots/English Dictionary to get a good close reading. It is well worth it though as this was not Socialist Realism as turned out by numerous other writers. The poem Chris mentioned on the Forum: A Drunk Man Looks at the Thistle is renowned for its synthesis of Scots dialects with some English language. He was a giant of a poet by any estimation and considered to rank with Robert Burns in Scotland. He created a new poetic, a counter-hegemonic:
 "Lallans language," which he used as the language of his early poems. Using the Scottish dialect, absorbing the quintessence from the long

tradition of Scottish country people, with the poet's modern sensibility which developed under the influence of the works of Mallarme, Rimbaud, and Rilke to correct any tendencies toward anarchism, these poems broke away from the English literary tradition and struck against the "English ascendancy" while displaying the brilliant genius of the Celts. This is the key element that makes MacDiarmid's lyrical poetry fresh and powerful.

-        Zuoliang, Wang (1984) "Reflections on Hugh MacDiarmid," Studies in Scottish Literature: Vol. 19: Issue 1.

MacDiarmid made an oblique but unfortunate reference to Trotsky in Three Hymns to Lenin (1957):
Trotsky – Christ, no' wi' a croon o' thorns
But a wreath o'paper roses.
                              - MacDiarmid (1957), p.13

An attack on Trotsky would be consistent with the Stalinist 'line' of the CPGB when it appeared in Second Hymn to Lenin which was written in 1932. However, MacDiarmid was a complex poet, and many of his comrades in the CPGB said, 'they did not know what to make of him?' He was expelled from the CPGP twice. He had been influenced by the ideas of John Maclean. Still, with Maclean's death and the receding tide of class struggle in Scotland [both believed Scottish Socialism would predate any British workers state], his ideas were less anchored. Although I agree with most critics, he was the most important Scot's poet since

Robert Burns but was not quite in Brecht's category as a Leftist poet.

Hugh MacDiarmid: Three Hymns to Lenin, was written at the zenith of his literary powers. They were certainly not facile Socialist Realism but profoundly complex works illustrating dialectic contradictions and attempted synthesise of the poet, of aesthetics and the Revolution. MacDiarmid was aware though of the paradox of the complexity of Modernist poetry and the language of the masses and he addresses this consistently. Bizarrely, I think, First Hymn to Lenin was first published in magazine form by the Rightist, if experimental poet and critic, T.S. Eliot in Criterion. The publication date of this collection in 1957 was not an accident. He re-joined for a third time the CPGB in 1956 and wrongly understood the Hungarian worker's revolution as a counter-revolution. Dismissing as 'sentimental' those who left the Party in protest at its suppression. MacDiarmid asserted what kind of poetry he wanted:

It only remains to perfect myself in this new mode. This is the poetry I want – all I can regard now as poetry at all, as poetry of to-day, not of the past, A Communist poetry that bases itself On the Resolution of the C.C. of the R.C.P. In Spring 1925: 'The Party must vigorously oppose toughness and contemptuous treatment of the old cultural heritage as well as of the literary specialists. It must likewise combat the tendency towards a purely hothouse proletarian literature.

- Hugh MacDiarmid (CP1, 1978, p. 615).

Although I disagree with Nancy K. Gish (1984 p.126) commentary on MacDiarmid's overtly political poems. However, drawing on primary sources she does make some noteworthy points on his early sense of alienation caused by his advanced reading age, 'I lived in a different mental world altogether." [Lucky Poet, p.17].

First Hymn to Lenin is composed in what has become known as a Muckle Toon Stanza (Bold (1984 p, 146) rhyming abcbdd:

Christ said: "Save ye become as bairns again."
Bainly enouch the feck o' us hae been!
Your work needs men; and its worst foes are juist
The traitors wha through a' history ha gi'en
The dope that's gar'd the mass o' gi'en
The dope that's gar'd the mass'o folk pay heed
　And bide bairns indeed...

For now in the flower and iron of the truth
To you we turn [...]
...
But at last we are wise and wi' laughter tear
The veil of being, and are face to face
　Wi' the human race.

MacDiarmid, a festschrift, (1962) p. 85. Here MacDiarmid is writing about major questions like ideology as in 'false consciousness' and human emancipation because as Marx argued 'the ideas of the ruling class are the ruling ideas in society. 'The German Ideology. Karl Marx 1845

My close reading of Hugh MacDiarmid, Second Hymn to Lenin reinforced the recollection that this was not platitudinous material as some Leftist poetry of the period was but here MacDiarmid asks profound questions about the interaction of poets & poetry and the masses. However, as Bold (1984) p 146 notes 'it opens conversationally.' His use of regular and italicised fonts is impressive it contrasts with an abcb rhyme scheme:

Second Hymn to Lenin.
'Ah, Lenin, you were right. But I'm a poet,
(And you c'ud make allowances for that!)
Amin' at mair than you aimed at
Thou' yours comes first, I know it.

[...]
An unexamined life is no' worth ha 'in' [...]
- MacDiarmid (1957), p 12.
(The unexamined life is not worth living is a dictum supposedly uttered by Socrates at his trial for impiety and corrupting youth, for which he was subsequently sentenced to death, as described in Plato's Apology (1997, 38a5–6.) Here MacDiarmid effectively uses italics to indicate a change of both speaker to 'first person' and tone. I sometimes use elliptical lines for a similar purpose.
Are my poems spoken in the factories and fields,
          In the streets o' the toon?
Gin they're no', then I'm failin' to dae
          What I ocht to ha' dune.
[...]
'Haud on haud on; what poet's dune that?
          Is Shakespeare read,
Or Dante or Milton or Goethe or Burns?
          – You heard what I said.
               - MacDiarmid, (1978) vol 1, p 323).

MacDiarmid returns to the standard typology for the final stanza, and he created a feeling of continuity using the assonance of 'e' sounds:
Unremittin', relentless,
Organized to the last degree.
Ah, Lenin, politics is bairns' play
To what this maun be! (ibid).

The contrast between MacDiarmid's First & Second Hymns to Lenin and my poetry in No more will the creatures of Prometheus fail in their tasks (Revised) is substantial. Although we both experiment with genre-bending. MacDiarmid uses a regular stanzaic pattern of quatrains subjected by asides in italics when employing the first speaker personal voice while I attempt a synthesis of Whitmanesque verse, the poetics of engagement and a metaphorical density reminiscent of the Metaphysical Poets. However, there is agreement on the nature of the poetics: 'I am a poet; only fools ask me for logic, not life.' (Lucky Poet (1994) p. 415):

          No more will the creatures of Prometheus fail in their tasks (Revised).
A spark zigzags then you put a hand to cool the heat into this lake and your fingers
Became frostbitten and they just clawed us cruelly, the reaction we pose does not
 Require refrigeration rather a transformation from victims of timidity into blacksmiths
 Of molten metal, we fashion steel into objects of a collective Nemesis, instruments of Retribution;

once buried and hid until a new vanguard of Spartacus performs the stab, lances a swollen abscess of pus, it must be drained, those bare-foot doctors to inflict a necessary pain by incision, a wound with History's scalpel, these poets don't just wear the masks of Dantesque masquerade, our dreadful dream is a relentless concentration of beams like white energy into prisms, then rainbows of hallucination until we fill empty heavens with the laughter of Zarathustra.

Nigel Pearce (2011), Sisyphus: a celebration, London, Chipmunkapublishing Ltd with Arts Council England, p.33.

Here I reject Socialist Realism and attempt to 'defamiliarize' the class struggle. In Shelley's words, long before the Russian Formalists challenged Socialist Realism, 'Poetry lifts the veil from the hidden beauty of the world, and makes familiar objects be as if they were not familiar; it reproduces all that it represents, and the impersonations clothed in its Elysian light stand thenceforward in the minds of those who have once contemplated them […].' P.B. Shelley (1821/1840) A Defence of Poetry.A Defence of Poetry by Percy Bysshe Shelley | Poetry ...
In Third Hymn to Lenin MacDiarmid rejects stanzaic form and Synthetic Scottish otherwise known as Lallans and embraces an anglicised free verse. It is of significance that MacDiarmid provided an alternative title for his final hymn which was Glasgow Invokes The Spirit of Lenin. Here we can see the quasi-mystical error that

MacDiarmid falls into repeatedly. Its origins were in Maxim Gorky's concept of 'god-building' which he first applied to the novel Mother (1906) to strengthen the resolve of the Bolsheviks after the failure of Russia's 1905 revolution. Lenin always opposed this idea, and it is noteworthy that Mother became the exemplar of Socialist Realism after the 1934 International Congress of Writers in USSR. Indeed, in Second Hymn to Lenin there is a reference to an 'A greater Christ, a greater Burns' (1978, p. 86) which sustains the religious registers from First Hymn to Lenin:

Third Hymn to Lenin (extract).
'You turned a whole world right side up, and did so
With no dramatic gesture, no memorable word.
Now measure Glasgow for a like laconic overthrow!
On days of revolutionary turning points you literally flourished,
Became clairvoyant, foresaw the movement of classes,
And the probable zigzags of the revolution as if on your palm.
MacDiarmid (1957), p. 20

A thematic differential between MacDiarmid's political poetry and mine is that in the tradition of unorthodox or 'post'-Trotskyism I reject the notion of 'the cult of personality' as an aspect of the Stalinist School of Falsification. While MacDiarmid here ascribes clairvoyant powers to Lenin. He may well have had his finger on the pulse of History but there is nothing supernatural about that quality.

I like the way MacDiarmid used variants of Scottish dialects to undermine the colonial linguistic hegemony of Standard English. He wrote in Standard English on occasion. Hugh MacDiarmid was a complex person and often employed the phrase 'myriad minded.' It is also clear that he was influenced by Rilke's maxim: 'the poet must know everything.'(LP, p.67) There was not the vast chasm some saw in his ideological proclivities when one understands that he believed in a 'synthesis', another favourite word, of Scottish Nationalism and a form of Marxism. In this, he was in the tradition of John Maclean and by once removed that of James Connolly.

Although, unlike W. H. Auden's gloomy prognosis at the end of the 1930s that 'poetry makes nothing happen' rather as Christopher Caudwell (1970) Romance and Realism, pp. 137-38) asserted 'Auden had never accepted Marxism as a worldview'. Auden had in my view become introspective making a turn to Freudianism when confronted with the carnage of the Second World War. Rather Hugh MacDiarmid would sum up his position thus:

"I am . . . interested only in a very subordinate way in the politics of Socialism as a political theory; my real concern with Socialism is as an artist's organized approach to the interdependencies of life."

- Lucky Poet: Hugh MacDiarmid | Poetry Foundation

However, an article about Three Hymns to Lenin upon their publication and favoured by Hugh MacDiarmid was written by Mr Burns Singer in a literary magazine called Encounter (March 1957): 'To unite the delicacy of his lyrics with the violence of his propaganda has been the central undertaking of his life. It is this duality that has made him the greatest of Communist poets.' I would disagree here and rather follow those who like (Bold (1983) The Terrible Crystal p, 18) believed his 'poems... bear (some) comparison with Brecht.' Although for MacDiarmid:

In short, any utterance that is not pure
Propaganda is impure propaganda for
sure.
-The Socialist Poems of Hugh McDermid (1978) p,14.

MacDiarmid's use of alliteration with the repeated 'p' sounds is reminiscent of a Leninist agitator addressing a group of workers anywhere in the world. Repetition is a tool used successfully by MacDiarmid with assonance, alliteration and more generally. This is a potentially useful lesson for use in my authorial practice and may help with focus and, even, with Eliot's 'objective correlative' assist in correcting overly subjective poetry. Here is a prose-poem which was an attempt to achieve this:

The chess board consists of 64 squares, are you one? (Revised).
The chipped chess pieces, the pawns, chant their abhorrence at the smooth and uninterrupted movement of both a Rook and the Queen, at the

fatal power of the Kings demise which terminates their game, he was checkmated because of impotence and ineptitude, you didn't avoid being mated: the Grand Master who is reincarnated as a flea studies the game, metamorphosis's himself into sticky brown slime, He then oozes onto the board, only godless like the inexorable tides, The tacky mucus seeps its way into the pristine chequered surface. Did you lead a chequered life or as cramped as the pawns, chipped, and clipped, never raced from A8 to R8, only P-K4, an anticipated Opening and so is everything else, just predictable like the ticking of a chess clock, you 'play by the rules', 'stay on the board'; secure, its Death-in-life because the brown snot is caustic, it will erode you until drugged the only option is to plead for checkmate with these 64 squares.

-        Nigel Pearce (2011) Icarus Still Flies. London, Chipmunkapublishing Ltd, with Arts Council England p, 19.

As I previously argued once the Platonic Theory of Forms is rejected, we only know the poet through the prism of their brain's biochemistry across which poetry refracts. Poets with dopamine and serotonin imbalances know their work can be celebrated or decried as they are 'myriad minded' in the manner of MacDiarmid.

bibliography.
Bold, Alan (1983) Hugh MacDiarmid: The Terrible Crystal, London, Routledge & Kegan Paul.
Bold, Alan [ed] (1984) The Letters of Hugh MacDiarmid, University of Georgia Press.
Bold, Alan (1990) MacDiarmid: A Critical Biography, London, Paladin Grafton Books.
Caudwell, Christopher, (1970) Romance and Realism: A study in English Bourgeois Literature, Princeton, Princeton University Press.
Duval, K.D (1962) MacDiarmid, a festschrift, Edinburgh, K.D. Duval.
Feringington, Bob, Sherry, Dave & Boyce, Colm (2021) Breaking up the British State: Scotland, Independence & Socialism, London, Bookmarks.
Gish, Nancy, K (1984) Hugh MacDiarmid The Man and his Work, London, The Macmillan Press Ltd.
Law, T.S & Thurso Berwick (1978), The Socialist Poems of Hugh MacDiarmid, London, Routledge, Kegan Paul.
Macleod, Isabelle, and Pauline Cairns [eds] (2012) The Essential Scots Dictionary, Edinburgh, Edinburgh University Press.
Hugh MacDiarmid | Poetry Foundation
MacDiarmid, Hugh (1987) A Drunk Man looks at the Thistle, Edinburgh, Scottish Academic Press.

MacDiarmid, Hugh (1967) Collected Poems of Hugh MacDiarmid, New York, Macmillan Company.

Hugh MacDiarmid: Second Hymn to Lenin (Spring 1960) (marxists.org)

MacDiarmid, Hugh (1978) [eds] Grieve, Michael & W.R Aitken The Complete Poems of Hugh MacDiarmid vols 1 & 2, London, Martin Brian & O'Keeffe,

MacDiarmid, Hugh (1994) Lucky Poet, Manchester, Carcanet.

MacDiarmid, Hugh (1969) [ed] Duncan Glen] Selected Essays of Hugh MacDiarmid, London, Jonathon Cape.

MacDiarmid, Hugh (1957) Three Hymns to Lenin, Edinburgh, Castle Wynd Printers Limited.

The German Ideology. Karl Marx 1845

Pearce, Nigel (2011) Icarus Still Flies. London, Chipmunkapublishing Ltd, with Arts Council England.

Pearce, Nigel (2011), Sisyphus: a celebration, London, Chipmunkapublishing Ltd with Arts Council England.

Plato (1997) Defence of Socrates, Oxford, Oxford University Press.

Purdie, Bob (2012) Hugh MacDiarmid, Black, Green, Red and Tartan, Cardiff, Welsh Academic Press.

Riach, Alan (1991) Hugh MacDiarmid's Epic Poetry, Edinburgh, Edinburgh University Press.

Royle, Trevor (1985) The Macmillan Companion to Scottish Literature, London, Macmillan Press Ltd.

A Defence of Poetry by Percy Bysshe Shelley | Poetry ...

Tengely-Evans, Thomas (2022) The Shadow of Stalin, London, Bookmarks.

Trotsky, Leon, (1937) The Revolution Betrayed, Leon Trotsky's Revolution Betrayed - Marxists

Zuoliang, Wang (1984) "Reflections on Hugh MacDiarmid," Studies in Scottish Literature: Vol. 19: Iss. 1. Available at: https://scholarcommons.sc.edu/ssl/vol19/iss1/3.

An ekphrasis on Vincent Van Gogh Starry Night
https://artsandculture.google.com/asset/the-starry-night/bgEuwDxeI93-Pg?hl=en-GB

Vincent remains alive for the crazy people,
He guides as we stumble in the moonlight,
Those swirls are twirling during that night,
Can cast into cascades of thorny delirium.

That church, its steeple is not a phallus,
But sits in a blue painting, bold brushed,
As if the canvas were a dot of madness,
No bonds, without boundaries, so free.

Descend into Dante's Inferno or ascend to
Paradiso, the same as we are like a yeast,
Hell or Heaven are incarnate in the insane,
We pick up pen or gun, live or die, a choice.

But were you a Burroughs, his finger, your ear,
That cold syringe or a madhouse, maybe both?
You shot yourself at 37, William made it to 83,
But then he 'always went first', yet you died first.

We artists and writers have no concrete shelter,
Either we take those slings and slurs or a grave.

Bleach Bath: A poem employing T.S. Eliot's
'objective-correlative.'
A set of objects, a situation, a chain of events shall
be the formula of that particular emotion.
Hamlet and His
Problems. T.S. Eliot. 1921. The Sacred Wood ...

This bath was just a variation on a theme,
The big black boot and the clenched fist,
 Revolutionaries expect this, even us kids,
But their repertoire in their house of Care.

A welcome was written numerically '666.'
On that superintendent's forehead, S.S,
For an intense hour, you could cut the air,
A rat arrived; he locked me in a bathroom.

 'You're a good boy undress',
He had emptied some bleach into a bath,
 About four inches slightly diluted, 'get in,'
 He just drawls; 'All communists are dirty',

 Never saw him again; he was brought in
To teach me a lesson and soften me up,
 But it failed.

The incident still smarts and is unforgiven,
The red reaper will avenge these crimes,
Our Nemesis will flush rats out of sewers,
There is nowhere to hide from class justice.

For Ian (R.I.P.): a documentary poem.

For him, I still can weep hot tears,

Ian was a fresher from Cambridge,
His mistake was to take an acid tab,
But he did not then soar to Heaven
Or descend into the fierce, fiery pit.

No, Ian's giant brain was scrambled,
They brought him in to the hospital,
Wild wide eyes, but blessedly calm,
Will you sit with him: 'yes, of course.'

That crazy man, Ian, showed me how
To solve a puzzle, the cosmic enigma,
A pack of cards Ian placed randomly,
Every day in a different configuration.

But Ian began rebalancing his scales,
Singing those Leonard Cohen songs,
A guitar strummed, if slightly off-key,
We loved it, not noticing his repertoire,

So sad songs Ian sung, smile beguiled,
but the doctors discharged him too early,
Frequently he housed me as an orphan,
After dad ejaculated me as 'a damn red'.

We were two roamers of the labyrinth,
Our wings had melted, contorted gladly.
One dark dawn slapped him, he hung,
But Ian had left no note of explanation.

Part Two, The Writer in the World element.

1) Back cover for a future publication:

The dialectic is nowhere more apparent than in the art of writing, for the literary object is a peculiar top; this exists only in movement. To make it come into view, a concrete act called reading is necessary, and it lasts only as this act lasts. Beyond that, there are only black marks on paper.

- Sartre, J-P, (2010) What is Literature, p. 29.

Therefore, you, my reader, are the essential component of the dialectic, as writing would not come to life without you. This is a collection of poetry whose origins and nature are my love of writing and ideas. Thus, writing and reading are essential to my being and, ironically, contributed to my entry into the psychiatric system just before my 14th birthday but have sustained me throughout. Books and ideas were both an early love and haven in a troubled family. Aged eleven, I met an English teacher who introduced me to new poetry and then some university students; we debated many concepts and the relationship between writing and ideas. The increasing involvement with the crowd at the university made the fault lines at home particularly sharp. I lived in a bubble of writers, artists, revolutionaries, and many people who had simply renounced a conventional way of life; it suited me. I went to live in an avant-garde squat in London and was introduced to 'experimental art' such as 'happenings.' Poetry, radical ideas, and everyday life simply merged into a dream. Within a year, a period of involvement with psychiatry begun which has continued over time. However, I will never cease writing and discussing books and ideas.

It is now eighteen years since I almost died from a medically induced toxic state related to medicines prescribed for mental health issues. I have had thirteen books published by Chipmunkapublishing, which had Arts Council Funding until recently and gained several qualifications to add to the B. A (Hons) before the toxicity, a Certificate in English Studies at Warwick University, a Dip. H.E., a B.A (Hons) in Humanities with Creative Writing, a Masters in English with Merit and a Postgraduate Diploma in Humanities with Merit gained at the Open University. The doctors thought that once I had survived the toxicity, the only way ahead would be a sort of vaguely animated death in long-stay psychiatric Care. I have proved them wrong, which is not to say my body and mind have totally recovered but have illustrated that adversity can be overcome. When confronted with one's mortality in a palpable form, you either sink or swim psychologically: I swam. A desire to push the boundaries of both the creative and the intellectual is pervasive in my work. I know no other path than writing, studying, and the struggle for proletarian revolutionary self-emancipation.

This collection from Nigel encompasses his beliefs and loves and his true love, poetry. It is both broad and challenging. But his desire is to, paraphrase William Morris, have literature, freedom, and liberty for not the few but for everyone.

2) Writer-in-residence proposal for Springfield MIND.

Mission Statement:

The core product would be a magazine named: Wake your MIND, a magazine for poets, artists, storytellers, and thinkers who, for whatever reason, feel excluded from mainstream publications. My concentration is on those in the mental health system and associated substance misuse services. The magazine would not be willing to provide a platform for fascism, sexism, racism in any of its many forms or anti-LGBT+ material. It will be distributed free of charge as a paper publication in Warwickshire (U.K.). Actions speak as loudly as words; if you don't want to make art and literature into another commodity fetish, you should make it free. A commodity only exists as an 'exchange-value'; if you create a 'use-value', which is what a product is when removed from the capitalist marketplace, it, to an extent, negates the negatives attached to commodity production. This is what I hope to achieve. Although I accept that this can only be attained in a qualitatively different society, in the last instance. The magazine had run in an earlier incarnation online, but that co-editor is sadly deceased. He designed the Logo, and it would be fitting to keep it in memoriam.

Logo.

Experience and background.

I had previously had a residence and run a magazine at the forerunner of Springfield MIND, MID-Warwickshire MIND. I was both a volunteer and a service user at that time. My entry into the psychiatric system occurred just before my fourteenth birthday, immediately after I was detained on Section 1 and Section 3 of the Children and Young Persons Act 1969. Subjected to powerful medicines both orally and intramuscularly and Electro-Convulsive Therapy (E.C.T.). However, I did meet excellent doctors and nurses over the decades. I thought that as creative writing had been in my heart since the age of four, it would be appropriate to provide a platform for others. Also, having run creative writing groups at MIND and worked on magazines at Community Arts Workshop and a magazine with another deceased co-editor at the National Schizrophrenia Fellowship (now Rethink) called Fourth Dimension, I would be appropriately qualified for the role.

Funding:
1) Apply to Springfield MIND for funding.
2) I am willing to contribute to the costs to maintain the integrity of the Mission
    Statement as had previously at Mid-Warwickshire MIND.

Purpose:
To encourage and facilitate the writing of outsider poets and others, especially in the mental health services but not exclusively. I would also be interested in copy and artwork from the homeless population. This is because I recognise that the majority of that unfortunate group have mental health issues, and they would have been housed

in the long-stay non-acute wards in the now-demolished asylums. My intended purpose in running this residency at Springfield MIND would be achieved by allowing these poets, fiction writers and artists to see their work in print. Thus, this would heighten their profiles and lead to the destigmatisation of mental disability. It would also enhance the self-esteem of those published by Wake your MIND.

The Inferno and Beyond.

(a sequence of 'voices' from Council Care, psychiatry, and the counterculture).

Refuse to be an accomplice Don't lie - don't keep your eyes shut.
-        Simone Weil in Zaretsky, Robert (2021) The Subversive Simone Weil: A Life in Five Ideas. p, 39.

The Inferno and Beyond.

Introductory Summary.

My inspiration was derived from a diversity of poets: Sappho, Dante, Milton, William Wordsworth, William Carlos Williams, Brecht, Allen Ginsburg, Sylvia Plath, James Wright and others. Wordsworth importantly embraced 'the real language of men' Preface to Lyrical Ballads and an introspective turn in The Prelude. The concomitant rupture of Modernism in the early poetry of T.S. Eliot and Ezra Pound is equally significant. As was William Carlos Williams' response. His use of juxtaposing different types of text impacted my writing. While the 'confessional verse' of especially Sylvia Plath is a significant influence. I also agree with William Burroughs: In my writing, I am acting as a map maker, an explorer of psychic areas, a cosmonaut of inner

space, and I see no point in exploring areas that have already been thoroughly surveyed.
- William Burroughs in Chad Weidner (2016) The Green Ghost: William Burroughs and the Ecological Mind, p.7.

Finally, I also used closed forms in recognition of the impact of New Formalism. My vision is multitudinous as it befits one who has mental ill-health. This collection gives 'voice' to those who experienced Council 'Care', the psychiatric system and counterculture. I followed Simone Weil's advice, kept my eyes open, and observed.
Two hundred words.

On reading T. S. Eliot's (1953) The Three Voices of Poetry
In a lecture delivered in 1953, "The Three Voices of Poetry", T. S. Eliot said that "dramatic monologue cannot create a character". As his title implies, Eliot distinguishes between three voices of poetry. The first voice is that "of the poet talking to himself-or to nobody", and the second voice is that "of the poet addressing an audience", and the third "is the voice of the poet when he attempts to create a dramatic character speaking in verse".

Do I write poems for the daughters and sons of Moloch? Do I scribe verse for a leap in trade union consciousness? Do I write in several voices, as Eliot had argued in 1953?

One more for the men who flagellate alone,
boozed, Another for a woman who told me of her
fisted abuse, Lines for junk sick, and mad youths
who will die soon.

Some more for the good and bad psychiatrists
Who are caring for cash?
Yet do they spend it all on their lewd midnight
bash

Awash with a little more than drinky poos, yes, it is
coke,
Gives that sparkle, stare, and glare; the doctor still
smells of the night before, yet I guess that there
was no time to

CHANGE.

So, dish out the sedatives and do not forget to
take one

YOURSELF.

A Shakespearian Sonnet to Eleanor Marx. 1855 - 1898.

Tussy, so you could only be his incarnation, The heights and depths of heaving workers, A fatal flaw is a scar, a martyr's inclination, Sigh and feel; never be like leaden bankers. A Polish, Jewish, Irishwoman girl of the light, Organized the women and girls match strike, Will Thorn, who you taught to read and write, A comrade of William Morris (he did not fight).

You translated Ibsen for the benighted masses, Madame Bovary with that misogynist Aveling, He was death in life, a cobra biting your riches, So, strike he did quite like a snake with a sting. Your prussic acid and chloroform made dead, Your blood has stained our flag a deeper red.

Mother (Maxim Gorky) 1.
 An Ars Poetica study.

My mum had not perused the Gorky, Or marched the streets on May Day, Did not know of his bright Red Flame; she was an actress in the play of ivy.

My mother had not moved into the fray; the path I took was like a dawn sunrise. But, mum danced with veils and masks And deceived many who twirled blind.

I read Mother at the Party Congress, The comrades brought food, coffee, Kind folk, but I sat alone in a canteen, And fell in love with this boxed novel.

Then hoped that some red epiphany Would impact upon my sad mother, She, a woman of the night in a day, Who performed the bourgeois rituals,

While we made Molotov Cocktails, In Derry, Handsworth, and Brixton, The vanguardists without mothers, She lived in a closed, tightened net.

1 https://www.marxists.org/archive/gorky-maxim/1906/mother/index.htm

My mum had been making suicidal suggestions to me since I was seven.

Like Hugh MacDiarmid, my reading age was quite advanced. When there was no suicide attempt: I politely asked: 'Are you going to kill yourself, mum.'
The chilly reply: 'I was just letting off steam.' I had to grow up wildly, quickly upon fallow ground.
I understood as a child that she was entrapped in a cage called the family; Mum was a free spirit who should have lived in an artist's colony.

I would leave for the counterculture at age eleven,
fleeing what was a little more than a war zone; the
Fuhrer and Mater screamed at each other but with
a bellicose bellow against my ideas.

    Yet I loved her, and when the moon beckons,
    Dig with torn hands into her entombed heart.

Sonnet for my other lost (foster) family.

They did mistake a tear with Hegel's Idea, This bat
flew with no eyes, no illusion,
I came into their world without that fear, With
sounds at dusk, not any pollution. Then heat
roared until your brain boils, Dad was a
transmitter, like a Lukács, They had reaped their
gains and spoils, Your brain had farrows, prepared
a stash.

You were the type to make them look a twit, When
the epoch did not collapse, a clown You moved
into business; I almost had a fit, The tide had
turned, but you had not a frown. The group would
soon merely use your name; I thought that it was
more than just a shame

Lines on Brigitte M', a leading member of the
S.P.K (Socialist Patients' Collective).

A chill and steel grimace glares and stares From
the steel goblet from which she sips; substitutions
are easy in the class struggle; she didn't substitute
emotions with zeros.

Replace the proletariat with a vanguard? Never
replace authenticity with their shit; kill a
revolutionist with a gun or tablets, Yet they will rise
like your fear of death.

From this cup drunk Brigitte M, not the China tea-
services of the oppressor, She smiled as that red
wine of love Intoxicated her with a fantastic desire

To destroy daddy in every manifestation.

She was an incarnation, the realization, And
beatification of our red insurrection;.
her gun shot lemon butterflies of love.

Daddy, Daddy, you bastard, I am through - Sylvia
Plath, Daddy.

The Gym-Mat 'in Care.'
Holy, Holy the Fifth International [...]
- Allen Ginsburg, Howl.

S.S, the superintendent did not like politicos, At
least not red rebels in his Care institution; we were

several boys and girls, the minority; his tricks are
well known to his kind, to divide.

An Assessment Centre on a summer evening, He
sunk beneath the line of decency as we Expected
child-care officers arranged a bout, A gym mat
boxing gloves, two of us refused.

They whipped the other children into a mob of
jeers; we stood alone resolute for half an hour,
Comrade Then said: 'I am sorry, I have to hit you',
we danced,
Sparring then a blow landed, blood is red

Just as we were, so we shouted: 'Long live the
Fifth International.'
They were mute, aptly abashed and will soon be
smashed.

Ward 19 at Hollymoor Hospital, Birmingham,
1974.

Just about fourteen, and Fate had cracked The
bell, which had chimed a blunt o'clock, Discord in
my head for Ward 19 had a bed, And a comrade
detained in Care was sent.

A crazed creature kept hurtling at the walls; his
body had bounced off bruised and bled,

Again, again, this was not any game, I realised;
these were men; why was I a child confined?

I want to go back to the adolescent Unit, I plead,
Say that again, and you have another Largactil...
The last one, I swear, had almost killed me; it did.
No refuge on 19's on the T.V around 8.35 p.m.

The Mulberry Bush erupts as staff stand stare, But
Bedlam undulates just like the tidal ocean,
Skeleton staff rattled, and a church firebombed, A
burr of nurses and doctors maintained scales.

I was back in the Unit as most staff had returned,
There was a smell of fear, an atmosphere I noted.
Learnt names: Liam and Bernadette; Gerry
smiled.

Hannah on Ward 10 at Hollymoor Hospital,
Birmingham, 1975.

Hannah, you do not and cannot stop the wailing; it
has been weeks; still, the tears flow in torrents; I
am so sorry and would gladly sacrifice myself In
your synagogue to wash, absent your stains.

An orthodox Jewess, a jewel with mousy hair,
Something had snapped in Tel Aviv at age 19,
Went sky high and slept all the way to the U.K.,
The men are damned, used a nymphomaniac.

Their leering eyes would not see your mania,
Only what lust-dripping salivating lips desired; I
saw the damage they had wreaked at fifteen,
It created a lifelong loathing of that type of man.

What befell Hannah would remain a mystery; she
floated away one sultry summer evening. Family,
suicide, or those demons of Mossad, I Never
again saw Hannah with her mousy hair.

A poet becomes catatonic in a psychiatric hospital.

His body of dust is fleeing the squares of black to white, The black and white tiled corridors winding, with no end; His smooth veil of tissue was torn cast into a river of sand.

Writing is transience as it is trapped in a house of mirrors   With the Dead, who kiss with burnt words like bubbling acid,
It blistered his lips until poetry was left choked and silenced.

The remembrance of an attempt to abuse me in an asylum.

What a loon was Vic, the nurse; Nurse Goodall wore sharp suits,

He was bathing me, too ill to myself; I was out of the bath; talcum powder Kept going up and up my legs. 'If you try that on. I will put you through the bloody wall.'
He backs off, but two days later, alone in the male Common room. He grabs hippy hair and then pulls Me the room's width, saying, 'I'll show you what violence is.' It was my word against his status.
It would have been futile; Largactil jab awaited.

Like all victims of abuse had thought I was alone.
After all, he had given me some Rupert Brooke;
he was struck off and would be an early A.I.D.s
casualty.

They let him return, but I was not sad when he
died.

The House on the hill.

An ivy house on the hill for those with dreamy
dreams,
Or said anonymous gods who strode in dirty white
coats
Around the wards with even black and white tiled
floors,
A nurse said, 'you are a no hoper' I was reading
Sartre.

Tuesdays and Fridays, we were wired to the grid,
E.C.T.
Routine rather than diagnosis, fancy rather than
science.
My Child Care Order expired; they had to become
careful.
The attitude was abruptly altered, no jabs or those
shocks.

Metamorphosis: 'you are clever and creative', they
say,
'Try the Open University in 1988', have degrees
gained
 Books published; a tempest of a voyage remains
ahead,
 Many did not survive; each death is etched on my
heart.

I stand solitary, encapsulated by books, yet alive,
writing.

Asylum.

A house on that hill had close manicured lawns,
Summer kissed lawns, but it burnt the patients,
The long stayers had old clothes that did not fit,
The staff just sat nodding into each other's eyes.

The psychiatrists whooshed around as Dervishes,
          until exhausted sunk whisky,
They were Father Confessors in this purgatory.
You had better give up all hope once admitted.

No one had anticipated the coming demolition,
It became a housing estate; many are homeless.

A priest realised God is dead and mourns.

A deep chasm of coldness is beating in this
grinding Heart; here, lovers' warmth had ridden
like a dawn, He celebrated Mass,
transubstantiation, and libation.

Now he is standing stunned in torn vestments
Night has enfolded his soul, the sacrificial Rite Of
Winter, and frost has frozen into a river of ice.

Empty whisky bottles did say an awful lot more
Than he would have ever preached to his flock.

Hymn to the Mortality of the Nazarene.

The Void beckons like graves welcome the dead;
Mary weaves barbed Threads of wire, dark
mystery, to coronate her poet who moves forward,
To glance into an infinity of broken glass, her eyes
of smiles, circles of black, There were stains on a
bed, but it was here she washed the blood from
sheets; these tinges are bled in a cycle of betrayal
and love, the Sunset and Sunrise.

He wipes the tears of mortality from his eyes and
steps to look beyond the edge, A taunting
precipice; he howled, 'Father, Abba, why did you
let my corpse hang Among unclean men and
these anaemic women?' 'Mother, why did not your
blood Mingle with the blood flowing from my
wounds in my hands, in my feet, and side? You
blessed the wisdom of fools in the shifting sand,
that myopia of the deserts.'

This infant, the Lamb, is a man tuned into those
pulsations of Alpha and Omega.

He leaps into the Void to dance with the eternal
damned.

W. H. Auden visited us, patients, as a Christmas
Treat.

The applause of literate nurses and pampered
patients was deafening. The great poet tended to
the needy for a fee; he was not Christlike,
I wonder how much these people know about this
celebrity poet.

I rise: 'Spain c:1936 is wiped clean from your
repertoire because of ....' 'Who is that inmate',
snaps Auden, like a military Staff Sargent to
infantry, 'That is one of our more challenging
patients.' replies Staff Nurse, smirking, "Why did
you censor: 'the young poets exploding with
necessary murder.' And 'Yesterday, the song at
sunset/ The adoration of the Madman/ But today
the struggle." 'I will not be heckled by a lunatic,
that deluded nutter.'

A young doctor joins the melee: 'Mr. Auden, you
wrote those lines although I understand since your
conversion, they may indeed smart more than a
little.'

'You are all deranged. Doctors and patients, keep
your fantasies to yourself.' 'A first edition is a
textual proof.'
'You cretinous idiots, take that.' A non-
metaphorical pitcher of water is hurled across the
hall. It hits the senior consultant, who is soaked.

A chime of cheers cascades from first the patients,
a gaggle of giggles from those Student nurses and
then 'you seem a little overwrought from the
Professor, a pill
would put that right.'
'Get away from me; I am leaving.'

"Not so rapidly, W.H. You seem agitated; could I
venture in need of a little rest,
on Ward No.6,'
'How very Chekhovian of you, Herr Professor.'
'How foolish of you, Mr. Auden.'

Homage to Dylan Thomas.
Yet death did have some domain, Poets die
young, and some older, Dylan, your words went to
heaven, I was in love with a boomed poetry, Not of
stages or the world of fame, We would not be
mourned by dust, For that random thud of our
blood,
You are an immortal, poetic etching.

The turn to booze with a hazy gaze, Morphine
blued your gold mouth, But dear Dylan, these
poems are Not resplendent with a Welsh wit, Yet
trickle from tributaries of you, With notions of your
craft and art.

Dylan and Caitlin Thomas drink themselves into
oblivion,
Let us dance with our dream of death. Grasp
tightly together, tumble in tunnels, chanting to nil,
cloaked zero, and chaos until freed from this
frenzy of whirling fire.
We're stroked into sleep, a slumber of solitude.

Lines for Sappho.

Your heart is aflame with red desire, Those
offerings for a Helen of Troy, Are wilted as you
write of a lost lover, Gone in your imaginations of
flowers, She had wandered Aphrodite's grove,
You had stroked my Aphrodite's buds.

A voice as sweet as flute at dewy dawn, The
music wrapping your beloved's body, In her white
linen robes so pure like desire, On Lesbos the
Muses are singing with joy, You write a verse of
love, and lyres do play, Yet a night still wails the
song of loneliness.

I genuflected dumb before the poet's alter, And lay
my back onto a willow netted cover, For she is my
eternal Eolian Harp, I write.

Narcissi and Red Roses.

Gusts of wind were howling around this white
cube, a bare room.
I plucked veils of silver cobwebs from these
shrouded, stinging and bloodshot eyes,
A globe of green satin was rolling around the floor
in a mist of purple; at its burning Core was a
priestess of Aphrodite, one of those who serve the
cult of love on Lesbos, The isle where Sappho

sings her spells. She began to celebrate Mass; I
genuflected before her altar of withered narcissi,
an aroma of sandalwood
was weaving like dust blown across a calm sea,
this scent intoxicated our senses; my supplicant's
hands were cupped in the form of a chalice before
her,
she was peeling the petals from a red
Rose, they fluttered gently into a porcelain cup; it
shattered into jagged pieces.

A Villanelle on the consequences of Sylvia Plath's
first sighting of Ted Hughes.

Sylvia Plath could not stop cursing her writing It
was a mesh of death yet so divine,
Because she could never forget that first sighting.

One morning, Sylvia was faced with writing so
biting. She had to calm herself with some wine,
Sylvia Plath could not stop cursing her writing.

When she realised that the writing was exacting
She tried to focus on the pen line,
Because she could never forget that first sighting.

I tried to distract her with a strike of sun lightening
Said the mind she had was so fine,

Sylvia Plath could not stop cursing her writing.

Sylvia Plath decided to do something frightening.
The writing began to have a moonlit shine
Because she could never forget that first sighting.

As night drew on, her eyes were not enticing Her
mind had just begun to mime,
Sylvia Plath could not stop cursing her writing,
Because she could never forget that first sighting.

For Sylvia Plath.

I am in your repose and so rest glad,
In that speckled rose budded grave,
A tomb, the canopy of willows wept,
Your purple soul just embraced me.

My pen is interwoven in caresses,
An entombed fragrance so sweet,
Ablaze with your lips red, purple,
My pen has murmured with Eros.

It scribes 'poetry is the blood jet.'

Padraig Anraí Mac Piarais.1879-1916.

I rest without the dust of ages,
The grieves of my land lighter,
Now that the people listened,
And rebelled in the ballot box.

Anoint a bride and her groom,
Her land and his vaulted sky,
To walk to an alter so awaited,
My ring is placed on the land.

"The Fools, the fools, they have left us our Fenian
dead, and while Ireland holds these graves,
Ireland unfree shall never be at peace."
- Padraig Pearse.

Anna.

A blond goddess of the underground, of the revolution, My back would be crisscrossed with ecstasy scratches, Our first year crashed into that second, that Year Zero, Posed as an urban guerrilla, you sold out the struggle.

A very nice lectureship with all the trimmings; how do you Square the circle; perhaps you were always a little giddy, We were lost and bewildered, as no 'love in the struggle', 'Love is not enough; I need cash.' 'Goodbye', my reply.

The poem is composed while contemplating the coming harvest by the masses.

A harvest ready for our History's reaper, As we watch the death throes of Capital, It is dying while squirming and belching, The scythes grasped by the oppressed, Glistening steel catches the golden rays,
We have not forgotten the long dark nights of torment in homes, hospitals, and prisons.

The bourgeoisie are deformed, walking dead, Are mummified in the bondage of bandages?

Patients brandish the bayonets of Bolshevism, Hardened in the same foundries and factories As the unscabbarded swords of these masses, They

are of the same furnace, a collective eye, The
many in One omniscient gaze, we glared.

Us creatures are unbound, Herr Dr Frankenstein,
Prometheans who carry the fiery plague to the
rich, This is an antidote to all mind-numbing
medicines,
it is a revolution
To clear all that mind pollution of competitive
evolution, The rats break free of your maze Dr
Skinner, so exclaim: 'Oh no, they are misbehaving
like those 'Homo sapiens.'

Unrhymed Sonnet.

They had an iron heart walking straight By a
young girl in peril for her the street, There was no
lion heart chivalric poem, A lady of withered
flowers almost dead, They did not note the bum
deal attempt, She pleaded 'tip me one mate', 'no
way', Was his hissed reply, was she about 16?
Her silent scream, that sea of salt sobs.

This dumb poet had his heart ripped out,
I knew that girl thirty-odd clean years ago, Illusions
we never had as 'smack' we did; dreamscapes
have that shimmering logic, Entombed in a body
with no umbilical cord,
The dealer's grey grimace had severed it.

In the Laboratory.

Red tentacles are gripping the wasted wail of a
seething brain which writhes in delirium with a
rush, white light C H N10 15
Eyes hang loose, attached only by yellow threads
to grey sockets; they melted a millisecond ago and
now are dripping, Dropping by diamond drop into
a culture dish, the doctor makes a smear, Places
a slide beneath the lens of a microscope and
peers in, A banshee screams into her eyes; she
jumps back too late, The laboratory rotates into
concentric circles; it has become a
phantasmagoria; that pain had gone; the chemical
lights blazed, but she had lost her mind, insane.

 Note: C H N10 15 is the formula for
methamphetamine (Methedrine).

A meditation on Andy Warhol's 'Factory'.

Many had entered this company of the joyful and
mad because they wrote when amphetamine had
hammered. They were sucked into a dark room,
dragged in, then spewed out when in pain; some
fixed and rapidly wrote,
Others painted after a hit; some wailed their ink or
paint onto paper like orgasms of

A moon's second rising: others were green-eyed
with their claws extended, Scratching each other
in the desert and simultaneously drunk from an
oasis; their straight and profane families of
mistrust were crucified and sacrificed, Coffined so
permitting poets and artists to descend from their
cross without showing their bruised stigmata.

Some wandered and wised their way out, went to
labyrinths of communes as hashish
somnambulists, but alert; they kept a pen and
paper within reach. A Barbiturate bard had been
taught to fumble, stumble, and mumble; he claims:
'I can recall and write about their verse and the
hearse of that Methedrine Ark'.

'This is Doctor Death calling', my friend
had said.

(a prose poem).

The room had not been cleaned since this speed
binge began around nine months ago. It was a
mess; empty cartons of orange juice speckled the
floor as we had tried to maintain our health with
Vitamin C. All of us were mainlining in excess of
two grams of high-quality amphetamine sulfate
daily and nightly because we did not sleep. As you
may or may not be able to imagine, the line
between everyday consciousness and the surreal
becomes more and more blurred until it

disappears. Throw into that cauldron an array of psychedelics, and the unconscious was the realm in which we resided. Any poetry, which was written, and art created, was like an Ego in this ocean of Id. This state of mind was a desired consequence. Unfortunately, the scene was not only composed of writers and artists, but as time went on, even some of the creatives were beginning to degenerate into hedonism, but it was changing and deteriorating. One day or night, who knew, as they merged into one another, I saw a man, almost a skeleton with giant protruding eyeballs, his thyroid had gone, jack up a straight gram of sulfate, flush, fill the syringe with blood, whack the blood up as well. Still, he pulled back the white plastic plunger and filled the 'works' with blood again, leapt to his feet, and spurted the blood onto the white emulsion ceiling. It was really crazy, man. Another young man had been trembling in the corner with a blanket over his head and shoulders, making occasional whining sounds: 'give me speed, man, I need speed, man.' My friend with whom I had discussed everything from the Dhammapada to Nietzsche yelped: 'man, this is really far-in, you know what I mean.' I replied, 'far-out, man, just far-out.'

Then he was consumed by something; I had never known what possessed him,
maybe his brain had finally dissolved. He loaded several syringes with speed and
moved like a spectre around the shimmering room. He injected one after another and said each time: 'This is Doctor Death calling....'

On hearing of the death of a hippy.
Turn on, tune in, and drop out.
-Timothy Leary.

That herd were thronging back and forth; While I
rolled along the old academic slot, Not unaware of
a lime green undercurrent, The radar is still finely
tuned, so inevitably

Street woman flies along on crystal crutches. She
stops dead 'Arthur is dead morphine O.D.', Those
buttresses of ice melt, and we embrace, 'I am
going to see him in the chapel I am now.'

She is skimming heaven on crystal meth; how
Long has she got, I shake, for they are blessed;
he was a gentle shadow-man who always said,
The same lines about some Nirvana or I-Ching.

Each death is scratched on my heart; it bleeds.

A man became an egg; (a surrealist poem).

There was a spectral man who hid in a physical
frame; He roamed like a grounded vulture across
the concrete. There was no harvest of gold corn or
pleasant deer too

Inspire the poet here, only the arched acridness of
the herd, Junkies huddled in alleyways wailing
with their junk sickness, The thin and translucent
membrane formed herself around And the man
touched a tingling rebirth; she had encrusted

Herself but eggshells are thin,
Egg boxes never are quite right like paper-mâché
disintegrating in the rain; The shell shattered, so
she dissolved herself and became the yellow
yoke.

Already an artist with eyes like black oceans had
painted the egg in beautiful
gold and blue,
He ate this egg; a yolk flowed out dark as bitter
blood into the pen of the poet. That poet then
wrote like a serpent who has just been uncoiled,
tongue licking.

A beam of hope that year: on the curing of a
terminal physical illness.

A death pyre fire was a flame that burned
throughout two thousand, and fourteen,
The stench of my burning flesh accompanied each
breath, and essay any poem scribed,
I was intoxicated and revolted by the odours of my
post-addiction, this a dance of death, Thirty years
clean and dry, degrees,
poetry and prose published have all been so cruel.

A new treatment and the consultant had agreed. It
was like the rising sun aglow, fondling my brain
And stroking what was the darkest of our nights
Because this was not the Dark Night of the Soul,
No, it would have been the oblivion of the tomb,
For there is not any belief in resurrection here.

Together with the medics and new antivirals, New
dawn, the albatross flies from my ship.

The Bluebottle.

A blue bottle was buzzing so bloody loudly; Boris,
darling Boris, you have saved us all. It dipped too
low than desired for workers, Go away, hey ho,
buzz off away or... We spray the true-blue fly with
insecticide, no lift red swot and thwack twat take
that, the dustbin of History opens to the rest of that
          swarm.
Crawl flies, beetles, lemmings to your doom,   For
ours is the dawn, the morning and noon.

To an unnamed person.

In a country graveyard, there are many quenched words, The words of love and hatred and forgotten pleasures, The laments of the hollow Dead and their demented wails, And yes, words of love which remained spoken, silenced.

A family torn asunder by malicious powers, forces so darkly, You had wallowed in the unhallowed ceremonies of midnight, But play with fire, and you get burnt, but so do the innocents, A saccharine smile fooled so many, yourself but not a priest.

We say this incantation to exorcise those fiery Dante demons:
"Vade retro Satana."
As you had said: 'I can fool any doctor, but I cannot fool you.'

They should have enforced the leukotomy for everyone's sake, For your demons could not simply be cast into a herd of swine.

The tale of a mother and her son (a narrative poem).

The Prologue.
In our beginning was pitch, infinite darkness,
There Isis conceived this sun-dazzled Icarus, Isis,
my mother, a fountain of Spring, Winter's Frozen
wasteland, you wept me into a genesis, It was
here we feasted on fruit that fell from the
Sacred Tree, then staggering drunk
With love and hate, we embraced clouds of gold.
We settled on the border of this chiming Garden;
This dance was enacted before the silver Serpent,
Wanderers of the Psyche, mother, was a Jewess
of the soul rather than the blood.
Grasped my hand and guided me from the
Garden, There the Serpent's tongue had licked
shut our eyes, We roamed hazy peaks and
caverns of biting dreams, Until this child was cast
in a mould, set, yet still molten With lava that
spewed from the Fall's ancient volcano, This river
burned furrows in our minds, two souls which
Had journeyed alone were one in the fire, like
intoxication, We wandered with Psyche, who is
unfathomable love.

Icarus soared.
The awakening screwed into this sun-dazzled
Icarus; I wept as mother entered the labyrinth of
dazed lies, So leapt out of that snare, the trap of
enclosed terror,

Focused on the poetry of psychedelia and
joyfulness, Visions I saw in the sky and soul

whispered into the sun, I soared and caressed the
gaze of a Serpent of silver,
In suspended heaven, these waxen eyes had
melted, Dripped, and dropped by a crystal into a
sea of frosted glass. To freeze the milieu of those
"straights", they follow zero.
Mother dies.
The black clams of Time stuck onto mum's frail
body; those rusty chains of age and illusion bound
her mind. She spiraled inwards in an introspective
frenzy of sparks. As her autumn leaves were
blown into the chill of Winter,
I walked with her and her ghosts in that becalmed
odyssey. Slimy Sea monsters would rise and
frighten us; both children, Mum and I, would sit in
the House of Dementia; she sat hunched
And meditating on the coloured interwoven
threads of her memories, The wind blew her, that
crumpled paper Buddha, away into infinity.

The icebox: a prose-poem.

This is a box within a box, a world within a world,
and a house typical of many in suburbia. It is
brown-bricked, anonymous, and almost transmits
hymns of praise to some tarnished copper god of
mediocrity. In the kitchen of this house stands a
fridge; it looks white and prosaic. Open the fridge
door, and at the top on the right is a sky-blue
icebox; it has three white stars to confirm the
adequacy of its freezing capacity. Inside the

icebox is a rectangular tray divided into squares; each can be filled with water and frozen to produce the perfect ice cube. This can then be dropped into a frosted pink glass that wraps around it, fruit juice, and the ideal chilled drink. A son frequently opens the fridge door, pulls down the sky-blue icebox flap, and peeps inside. He examines the frosted walls, which, paradoxically, burn his fingers; they are almost burnt with the coldness. In this world of ice cubes, he discovers another dimension that exists separately from but is intrinsically attached to the ebb and flow of everyday life. The son's mother had died some years ago. The son had an unusual relationship with the ice cubes in the fridge, finding great comfort in popping two out from the tray and holding them in his hands until they were numb and the ice cubes dissolved into water. The living room of this box within the box was bare, with no carpet, furnishings, or pictures. However, glaring at him was a gas fire. It had short brown steel legs at each end to support it. A copper pipe stuck up through the floorboards and was connected to the fire. The fire was coloured in two tones of brown, light brown at the bottom and around the sides of the gas jets and dark brown above. The shelf, which was on top of the whole apparatus and rested against the wall, had white plastic knobs at each end; one was to turn on and ignite.

The other was to control the gas flow to regulate the temperature. This fire concerned the son greatly; it almost dominated him. He didn't like the hissing of the gas or the flickering flames, and the brief smell of gas at ignition caused him much anxiety. He felt little or no choice but to constantly check and check again that the gas was burning correctly and there was no leak. With the certainty of the tides, his life became enslaved to this gas fire. The only respite was allowing the ice cubes to melt in his hands. Just as the season's motion is inevitable, the gas fire developed a leak. Fortunately, the son was elsewhere when the explosion tore through the house, destroying it and its anonymity. It no longer looked like all the other houses in the cul-de-sac. The fridge was severely damaged and thought to no longer fulfil any practical task; it was taken to the local tip. The ice cubes turned into water, but a more profound metamorphosis occurred: a voice said: 'My son, there is no longer any need to worry.' The water had leaked from the icebox and out of the fridge into the rubbish of the tip in which it germinated as a seed planted at the beginning of Time. In Spring, the shoot may push its way up and bloom into pure snowdrops.

Will, the jackbooted ones, march through the tip and crush in blind But ordered fury this flower and any hope of its delicate flourishing.

I am breaking down and breaking through.

When we can see beyond the tokens of things, To penetrate those masks of men and women, And lift those veils that most are hidden behind, A child with an all-devouring mouth and eyes.

This collapse could renounce a communicant's
Belief in the Host and hurl into Dantesque hell;
Here, we will meet forgotten selves and ghosts,
Twisted in agonies of reabsorption into the ego.

But a doctor, not today a priest, may intervene,
That keeper of the profane apothecary exorcise,
Unlike Hildegard, Julian, those medieval mystics,
We are not celebrated but are instead shackled.

For today there is not the adoration of madmen;
instead, the projection of your fears onto them.

Autumnal.

This season of mellow fruitfulness, the apples
were teeming with termites, That Tree who held a
fruit of temptation called knowledge is now rotten,
Earth, whose roots clasp and grasp, is frozen like
a leaden bronze sky.

Adam lies in the depths of a cider vat; he had
waved, drunk and drowned, The leeches replace

manacles on his mind, and his body is now wormed,

A howler of hurricanes tossed the loose leaves; laughter was lost too soon, The woman who kicked her way through the shades of brown and crimson, She fled in a flurry of rustling colour, and Eve escaped the Garden gladly.

No verse is free for the man who wants to do a good job.'
   - T. S. Eliot (1957) On Poetry and Poets, p.37.

Lines on writing poetry through the prism of
schizo-affective disorder.

My poetry can fling into flights of flurries, any
figurative phantom,
                    Demon, Ghoul, Ghost or Spectre,
I wrenched these words from a brain seething with
purple worms,
Those 'mind-forged manacles' melt like icicles
without my volition.

It is into that prism
 this wild poetry must be...
Refracted through an undulating optic of a
preordained iconoclast,
To make this unmade poetry into something so
precise, ordered,
I must ease my mind into a straitjacket, a mould of
concrete, clay.

Now, these devils, ghouls, ghosts, and spectres
become coaxed
Into The Common Reader, but I am not in Virginia
Woolf's class,
She was born above me in both wealth, status and
was a genius.

Note. Woolf, Virginia (2003) [ed] Andrew
MacNeille, The Common Reader Vols 1 & 2
London, Vintage. These were a collection of
literary essays initially published in 1925 and
1932, respectively.

Studies in syllabics.

Winter Haiku.

Ice has formed across
A lone pool, words are crying
Beneath its smooth face.

Haiku in madness.

Madness exhales breath
To lift veils, there the sane gasp
For they have no air.

Two classes, two poetics, a Marxist Ars
Poetica.
   'Understanding the poem is not only an
intellectual act but a political act.'
-        Frantz Fanon, The Wretched of the Earth.
They seem like an eagle, then swoop
 Like a vulture in search of its carrion,
The width of that cloth matters to you
 As you blather with pounds sterling.

You pose with a jewel-encrusted pen
Which is dry, no ink oozed from its nib,
We forged a nib of the masses in steel
With lightning strikes and thunderclaps.

Writes on papyrus, parchment, and paper,
The internet also hums as part of this kit,
We have many pens, but who holds them?
Scribes, sleepers, scholars, and workers.

One History but two classes, two poetics,
They clash with sparks; they are cymbals
In History's echo chamber, softly or noisily,
Then the Albert Hall crumbles as we sing

Until we are no longer like Robinsonades,
But resonate with a verse woven by us all,
So, multiplicities of pens write on the page,
This is the linen soaked in blood, our flag.

For whom the bell tolls. (A political poem).
> Perchance, he for whom this bell tolls may be
> so ill, as that he knows not it tolls for him.
-        John Donne.

Etonian bankers bark orders wrapped in gold leaf,
In vestments of Capital, the suits with twisted ties,
Lays with defrocked priests, a smirking Pharisee,
But sighs with a pleated moan in Downing Street.

Britannia tacks in choppy seas with winds
groaning,
Beware because you are not a mirage,
anachronism,
The lava of the oppressed is bubbling up in
oceans,
It will sweep the dust out of that empty opera
house.

Bourgeois end that obscene ballet with cut-out
dolls,
You are now dancing with terrible tolls of death
bells,
Begins to ring in their ears, weep, wince, and
whine,
As the proletariat strikes, a black panther on its
prey.

Panther's patrol streets the vanguard of red stars,
People live freely now as dollars have burnt, died,
The oppressors are tin soldiers who had rusted,
The Festival of the Oppressed is like a rainbow.

Let those living dead return to their catacombs,
While we fill these wineskins with clean waters.

A detained teenage political prisoner in a
psychiatric hospital in the 1970s.

A poem of witness.
A monk on another ward also conversed on Tim
Leary and Che, so we colluded,
Nurses without eyes, just film covered ones

Presumed purveyors of darker arts,
This poet wrote in metaphors not grasped by

those who had crawling sedated minds,
Doctors had theories as children are born
in bell-jars of discontent, no need to worry.

Then clientele spat sputum into cardboard

Spittoons not emptied, but flung in rage,
Doctors hid them in wards with sycophants

Faces like brick-and-mortar monotone,
A nurse wanted patients to be aborted cherubs of
heaven. But were like banshees,
No one dared mention the death of a young victim,
as things were hot in those hells.

'Take over the asylum and make it a red campus':
howled the interned revolutionary,
Just play bingo, pleaded Janus nurse as he
winked at some wincing nurse students,
The patients leapt like tigers, so that panzer squad
prepared a spikey chemical cosh,
All had electro-convulsive therapy called Terror
afterwards as the wires just buzzed.

Not forgotten were those whose deaths in
Stammheim Prison had left a bitter taste,
Ulrike, Gudrun, and Andrea's suicide in the
securest prison ever built, possibly not,
Bitter is a taste of lemon; lemon is yellow that will
colour if cancer strikes in the liver,
Red is our funeral shroud because cowardice
does not glaze those jaundiced eyes.
Note 1. "red campus" during the early 1970s, the
orthodox British Trotskyist organisation,
International Marxist Group, adhered to a position
that if they gained control of the universities. It
would then be possible to spread the revolution to
the proletariat.
Note 2. Ulrike Meinhof, Gudrun Ensslin & Andreas
Baader were founding members of the West
German Leftist urban guerrilla group, Red Army
Faction. They died in suspicious circumstances
within Stammheim high-security prison, which
housed RAF prisoners.

Commentary.

The course material suggests that poets often try to identify the zeitgeist of an age. I prefer Althusser's model of the 'problematic' because it complexifies what is a generalization:
 A word or concept cannot be considered in isolation; it only exists in the theoretical or ideological framework in which it is used: it's problematic. It should be stressed that the problematic is not a worldview. It is not the essence of the thought of an individual or epoch which can be deduced from a body of texts by an empirical, generalising reading; […] it can therefore only be reached by a symptomatic reading (lecture symptomale q. v) on the model of the Freudian analyst's reading of his patient's utterances.
https://www.marxists.org/glossary/terms/althusser/index.htm

Althusser, however, used his theory to show an 'epistemological break' between the 'Hegelian Marx' and 'Mature Marx.'
    How does one apply these ideas to poetry today? Adam C. Woodruff (2002) provided an insight:
            Eliot's persistent drive towards impersonation echoes (an problematises) the efforts of Benjamin, Lucan, and Althusser
to construct a model of the social process that incorporates the unconscious.

I therefore argue first that Althusser's 'problematic' resonates with T. S. Eliot's theory of 'impersonality' in poetry and, second, with his concept delineated in Tradition and the Individual Talent (1919):

> 'No poet, no artist of any art, has his complete meaning alone. His significance, his appreciation is the appreciation of his relation to the dead poets and artists...'

> (PDF) Tradition and the Individual Talent' (1919)

This is self-evident in modern conceptions of intertextuality. Here is my skeletal aesthetic. I would augment this position with an observation made by Karl Marx:

> The social revolution [...] cannot take its poetry from the past, but only the future.

Therefore, in circumstances of societal transformation, the conditions for the writing of poetry would be altered. So, given a different problematic, the social and unconscious forces would be unique. Therefore, my poetry both describes dashed hopes, but also expectations.

Nevertheless, what of 'my art and craft' to coin Dylan Thomas' phrase. The quintessence of my writing is that it is refracted through a mind which has both dopamine and serotonin imbalances or, in the language of psychoanalysis, 'the unconscious'. I describe this in the first poem of my cycle. What does this mean in practice on the page? Although I may edit rigorously, almost like a shoal of piranha fish turning on itself. The material must invariably remain coloured by metaphor, simile, and concept. This is not a conscious choice, and I try to employ countervailing measures, but its core is biochemical. However, I would hope that it is, to an extent, tempered by poetic technique gained at undergraduate, during the Master of Arts in English (2019) and in the current MA Creative Writing. Hopefully, my material transcends the nebulous world of autodidactic 'outsider art.'

My tutor has been of substantial assistance, particularly in an edited exchange of emails posted on the Tutor Group Forum. He encouraged me to use fewer metaphors and employ items from the News and 'nitty-gritty' symbols. I have tried to implement this, especially in: For whom the Bell Tolls, by using proper nouns and relating them to images, and found this a rewarding experience. I have attempted to replicate this advice throughout this piece of work.

Bibliography.
Althusser, Louis (2005) For Marx, London, Verso
Books.
Althusser, Louis,
https://www.marxists.org/glossary/terms/althusser/
index.htm
Althusser, Louis and Balibar, Etienne (2009)
Reading Capital, London, Verso Books.
Brecht, Bertolt [eds] (2015) Kuhn, Tom and
Constantine, David The Collected Poems of
Bertolt Brecht. London, WW Norton & Co.
Berlina, Alexandra [ed] (2017) Viktor Shklovsky, A
Reader, London, Bloomsbury.
Callinicos, Alex (1978) Althusser's Marxism,
London, Pluto Press.
Cook, Jon (2004) Poetry in Theory, Oxford,
Blackwell.
Donne, John (2012) [ed] Bell, Iona, John Donne
Collected Poetry London, Penguin Classics.
Eliot, T. S (1919).(PDF) Tradition and the
Individual Talent' (1919)
Eliot, T.S. (1957) On Poetry and Poets, London,
Faber & Faber.
Forche, Carolyn and Wu, Duncan (2014) [eds]
Poetry of Witness: The Tradition in English 1500-
2001, London, WW Norton & Co.
Frank, Robert & Sayre, Henry (1988) [ed] The
Line in Postmodern Poetry, Chicago, University of
Illinois Press.
Freud, Sigmund, (2006) [ed] Adam Phillips, The
Penguin Freud Reader (Penguin Modern
Classics).

Marx, Karl (1852)
https://www.marxists.org/archive/marx/works/1852/18th-
Marx, Karl & Engels, Friedrich (1968) Selected Works, London, Lawrence & Wishart.
Oppen, George (1981) Selected Poems, New York, New Directions Books.
Suvin, Darko (2020) Communism, Poetry: Communicating Vessels, University of Toronto, Political Animal Press.
Thomas, Dylan (1971) Collected Poems 1934-1952, London, Dent & Sons Ltd.
Wilkinson, Den (2021) Don Paterson: Readers and Writers, Liverpool, University of Liverpool Press.
Williams, Carlos William (1969) Selected Essays, New York, New Directions Books.
Woodruff, A.C. (2002) 'I Caught the Sudden Look of Some Dead Master': Eliot's Tradition and Modern Materialism', Culture, theory and critique, 43 (2), pp. 85–100.) https://pmt-eu.hosted.exlibrisgroup.com/permalink/f/gvehrt/TN_cdi_crossref_primary_10_1080_1473578022000038027
Wiegers, Michael (2003) [ed] This Art: Poems about Poetry, Washington, Copper Canyon Press.
Woolf, Virginia (2003) [ed] Andrew MacNeille, The Common Reader Vols 1 & 2 London, Vintage.

A poem in Blank Verse upon reading Tara Bergin:
The Tragic Death of Eleanor Marx (Revised).
'Understanding the poem is not only an intellectual
act but a political act.'
      - Frantz Fanon, The Wretched of the Earth

A cloth with width is what matters
Because you seethe with dollars,
As you are lost, then seek trophies
As vultures search for their carrion.

A jewel-encrusted pen you posture
With is dry, no ink oozed from its nib,
The nib of masses is forged in steel
In bloody sounds with a thunderclap.

It writes on papyrus, parchment, paper,
The internet is also a willow in the wind,
We have many pens, but who holds them,
Scribes, sleepers, scholars, and workers.

One History but two classes, two poetics,
They clash with sparks, as are cymbals
In History's echo chamber, soft or noisily
Until the chamber crumbles, a new song.

Then we will not be like Robinsonades,
But resonate with a verse made by all.

Ivan Dmitritch Gromov on Ward No.6 in the
asylum. (a prose/concrete poem).

My name is Ivan, and I address you from a ward in
the asylum. I was merely sat huddled in an
overcoat observing a streetlamp; it was hanging
with my mind from the moon.

This room is like a block of ice,
 A pixilated light is scolding my eyes
 I pick up my blanket and try to block out the
moonshine,
Because the moon is scornful of my mind,
I remove this rag of a blanket; the lunar light
glimmers again and bounces off these walls; it
drowns me. Morning

 Mutters outside the room. A big polished black
boot kicks open the door and crush me as if I were
a piece of origami. There is also pelting sleet
outside
That burns me like the pain from the blow of that
boot,
It burns like the Sulphur in Dante's Inferno.

It is finger-numbingly cold in their inferno.
They may believe I have a torn and twisted heart.
No, it is not cold but convoluted and complex like
a puzzle. I run from this room, feel the water, and
feel the rain, icy as if spurting from a frozen geyser
in Siberia. Fall to the ground, the Earth, with a
splat. I am instantaneously frozen. I was never in
any doubt that their heart was true blue, cold like
the sky hanging across Antarctica.

My body had been forcibly frozen.
Once placed in a crossbow, a steel arrow can
pierce the hottest soul in a stiff straitjacket. When
this bolt haemorrhages those blue people, they
will be as if nothing pure zero.
That foul smell of decay in a wilderness,
Which will be blown away by a wild wind,
Dr Andrey Ragin, join us in this struggle,
      Now, you have no choice in the asylum.
You see the peril of reading Chekhov.

Two poets contemplate Salvador Dali:
The Persistence of Memory. (An ekphrasis).
https://www.moma.org/collection/works/79018
Their mind is opening like a
lotus flower stung

By a spear of reed,
her breath drifts in lemon

Globules, pupils are fixed on
 a door which is woven

From willow branches, he opens an
aperture to discover

A zone that interacts
with her black eyes, leaden

In the midst of lunar storms, they
embrace, bodies are like

Cotton pages blown across a sea covered in silver
scales, until wrapped

In a ball of silk, they exhale rhythmically
with the pulse of the Earth, the clock faces have
melted.

A Shakespearian Sonnet to a modern Mary Magdeleine.

Their breath was silk and choked with sin,
Her gloss black boots of leather mock him,
A fascist complete with a whip to discipline,
He curls into a ball before the bloody hymn.
That strap was raised just like a Nazi play,
It cracks with whacks like goose-step troops,
They do not love like sheep who come Sunday,
But you and I know the song of our troupes.
Our Lady of Sorrows forgot to shut the bars,
Had drunk with those sad, mad, and bad men,
But fell on streets to gaze at dim-lit mist stars,
Tried Mass but heard Nietzsche's madman.
If God is dead, mirage, you have a vocation,
Maybe shadows of fire whisper edification.

Commentary.

These poems originated in both coursework and my independent research and the sparks which flew off both. Firstly, Two classes, two poetics was derived from my reading of Tara Bergin (2017) The Tragic Death of Eleanor Marx and Darko Savin (2020) Communism, Poetry: communicating vessels. These drew on an interest in anti-Stalinist Marxian socialism, which is long established in my reading. Although, not to the exclusion of other influences. Three Marxist poets appeared to have dominated Red Modernity, Vladimir Mayakovsky (who shot himself rather than become a spokesperson for the Stalinist counter Revolution), Bertolt Brecht, who wrote around one thousand poems and found himself trapped by the Cold War and Hugh MacDiarmid, who was expelled from the Communist Party Great Britain three times for petty-bourgeois Scottish Nationalism. I am pointing out that poets are frequently drawn to the Left but often feel uncomfortable in that culture. Marx articulated this position in a conversation with Eleanor Marx regarding Heinrich Heine:

He loved him just as much as his works and was as indulgent as can be towards his political weaknesses.

Poets, he declared, are peculiar people. You cannot measure them with the usual scale for normal people.

- Eleanor Marx: Neue Zeit.

It is a Marxian Ars Poetica but intends to transcend Socialist Realism which Trotsky argued against. It harnesses techniques appropriate to Blank Verse in this line with an iambic pentameter employing both alliteration and assonance:

It writes on papyrus, parchment, paper

[...]

The repetition is intended to beat the march of History, and the assonance promoted a sense of pervasiveness. This technique was gleaned by my reading of Mayakovsky's later poetry in translation.

Ivan Dmitritch Gromov on Ward No.6 in the asylum was evoked in the first instance by the course materials on the prose poems and the concrete poem. The latter with the employment of white space and varied typography and lineation of text on the page and thus on the visual impact of the poem. It is intertextual in that it alludes to Anton Chekhov Ward No.6. The 'bolt' is reminiscent of the regular use of intramuscular Chlorpromazine on psychiatric patients in the 1970s. Unlike Two Classes, two poetics relies, to an extent, on Christian registers or iconography. Also, this seminal quotation from Baudelaire was of inspiration:

Which of us has not, in his ambitious days, dreamed of the miracle of poetic prose, musical without rhythm and rhyme, supple enough and choppy enough to fit the soul's lyrical movements, the jolts of consciousness?
- Charles Baudelaire, (1970), Preface to Paris Spleen, p. ix-x.

Two poets contemplate Salvador Dali: The Persistence of Memory (an ekphrasis) arose from a concept in my imagination sparked by the discussion on visual poetry in the course material. Also, reading Freud on the creative process drew parallels between creating poetry or other art and daydreaming where memory is brought into consciousness.

My Shakespearian Sonnet emanated from reading Charlotte Mew (1916) Magdalene in Church. I was writing against the genre while understanding John Donne's sacred and secular sonnets, Mew's poem, and Don Paterson, 40 Sonnets. All four poems, self-evidently, exhibit shifts in authorial tone.

Bibliography.
Barry, Peter, (2013) Reading Poetry, Manchester, Manchester University Press.
Baudelaire, Charles (1970) Paris Spleen, New York, New Directions Books.
Bergin, Tara (2017) The Tragic Death of Eleanor Marx, Manchester, Carcanet Press.
Brecht, Bertolt, (2019) Collected Poems, London, Norton & Company.
Carson, Anne (2017) Short Talks, London, Brick Books.
Chekhov, Anton (2002) Ward No. 6 and Other Stories, 1892-1895 (Penguin Classics), London, Penguin Books.

Clemens, Brian and Dunham, Jamey (2009) An Introduction to the Prose Poem, Western Connecticut State University, Firewheel Editions.

Cousins, A.D & Howarth, Peter [eds] (2012) The Cambridge Companion to the Sonnet, Cambridge, Cambridge University Press.

Copus, Julia (2019) Charlotte Mew, Selected Poetry and Prose, London, Faber & Faber.

Copus, Julia (2021) This Rare Spirit: A Life of Charlotte Mew. London, Faber & Faber.

Donne, John (ed) Robbins, Robin (2010) The Complete Poems of John Donne (Longman Annotated English Poets). London, Routledge.

Duffell, Martin, J (2008) A New History of English Metre, London, MHRA.

Fenton, Frantz (1965) The Wretched of the Earth, London, MacGibbon & Kee.

Freud, Sigmund (1985) Penguin Freud Library, Volume 14. Art and Literature. London, Penguin Books.

Harrison, Tony (2007) Collected Poems, London. Penguin Books.

Hetherington, Paul and Atherton, Cassandra (2020) Prose Poetry An Introduction, New Jersey, Princeton, Princeton University Press.

Hirsch, Edward (2014), A Poets Glossary, New York, Houghton Mifflin Harcourt.

Law, T.S. & Berwick, Thurso, (1978) The Socialist Poems of Hugh MacDiarmid, London, Routledge, and Keagan Paul.

Levin, Phyllis [ed] (2001) The Penguin Book of the Sonnet, London, Penguin Books.

Longenbach, James (2018) How Poems Get Made. London, W.W. Norton & Company.

Marx, Eleanor Neue Zeit.
https://en.internationalism.org/icconline/2007/march/heine

Mayakovsky, Vladimir (2015) Mayakovsky, Volodya: Selected Works, London, Central Books.

Mew, Charlotte (1929) The Farmers Bride, London, The Poetry Bookshop.

Noel-Tod, Jeremy (2019) The Penguin Book of the Prose Poem: From Baudelaire to Carson, London, Penguin Books.

Paterson, Don (2012) Selected Poems, London, Faber & Faber.

Paterson, Don (2015) 40 Sonnets, London, Faber & Faber.

Roberts, Phil (2000) How Poetry Works, London, Penguin Books.

Ruhle, Jürgen (1969) Literature and Revolution: A Critical Study of the Writer and Communism in the Twentieth Century, London, Pall Mall Press.

Savin, Darko (2020) Communism, Poetry: communicating vessels, University of Toronto, Political Animals Press.

Trotsky, Leon (1992) Trotsky on Literature and Art, New York, Pathfinder.

Voronsky, Alexandr (1998) Art as the Cognition of Life, Selected Writings, 1911-1936, Michigan, Mehring Books.

The Tenth Muse in a man's world: responses to
Patriarchy in poetry.

A Sonnet (Shakespearean) for Anne Sexton.

Those hands began to write a page with dew,
Her heart had shed the haunts and bonds of Light,
She turned and smiled to cast a spell, this guru,
So tense until her pen began to write…
A verse of storms, angels of night who share,
Her seas of lavender wept waves of wonder,
The sun had raised so redly to kiss her hair,
She sat quite still and breathed like Buddha.
Her wine could sweeten bitter potions,
But doctors, the priests of modernity
 Are glaring flames; her poems were emotions,
They scorched them with shocks of electricity,
These burnt into her heart of love, your mind,
 A soul was numbed by barbiturate and lay blind.

Nigel Pearce

For Elise Cowen (1933-1962), a Shakespearean Sonnet.

Your smile it shone with clouds we call our verse,
You glimpse the straights in cars with an iris blur,
And gaze at Forms they drive in their cracked hearse,
For you who dance stark words without murmur.
The peace of wombs was like a coiled temptress,
Our wastes we walk without that veiled humour,
A moth flew into the night which was sadness,
A flame that burnt your wings had no candour.
I cupped and scattered you in morning dew,
You wrote the lamentations of the desert,
A mind was sane in that cruellest mildew,
The strength in the syringe was just like dirt.
It is here that some lie stillborn in the womb,
I dig in graves in search of your lost tomb.

I was Simone de Beauvoir's lost child.

I was made for another planet altogether. I mistook the way.

— Simone de Beauvoir, The Woman Destroyed, 1969.

My mother and I ached with the beauty of Beethoven, which caressed our minds,

Where else could an Appassionata Sonata be
played but bliss in those heavens,
Aphrodite chained to a cruel cross, yes, our love
was crucified, and it bleeds red,
Neither of us was of the world, which we assumed
belonged to ghost nightmares,
We celebrated our love of poetry and philosophy,
you Muse of past, the present,
My wings, contorted wax had whipped up a
tempest that you thought so terrible,
That you and your butterfly heartbeat for me
fluttered away one summer's night,
It went straight back to the planet forsaken and
drowned in a sea of gold coins,
An ornate veil hid a petrified perfection that brute
with the boot and book bought.

Now my mind screamed, and blood runs sour as
there is no beebread to nourish,
I am an amphibian without wings, gliding, sliding
through endless waves of pages,
Solitary creature shunned by a world, a hermit in a
wasteland of theses and writing,
This slime is like primaeval sludge

                              for Leary gave
the trips, Sartre the amphetamine,
Leary would mangle the world, Sartre 'lit up his
mind', your ideas were like lightning.

Summer of love, 1967. (a neo-villanelle).
Time melts thawed a frosty reality to dissolve ice without a stumble,
Our eyes, whose dilated pupils could swallow any hardened gaze,
(You fell across this hallucinogenic Cosmos, those stars humble).

We crucified the betrayal of damned love and stared so terrible,
That dark spark we conceived was like evaporating into a haze,
Time melts thawed a frosty reality to dissolve ice without a stumble,

I touched with delicate fingers the clasp on your eyes to unbuckle,
A stream, the purple fragrance of humming, a goddess was ablaze,
(You fell across this hallucinogenic Cosmos, those stars humble).

You crumpled in a sphere of sighs encircled by Light only to sparkle,
Whose wings were caressed, and we dived into the sun in a daze,
Time melts thawed a frosty reality to dissolve ice without a stumble.

Our song was vibrating into weeping trees, nectar dripping, suckle,
The other's ancient milk, which is a sacred libation with our praise,

(You fell across this hallucinogenic Cosmos, these
stars humble).

Tangerine gasp intertwines in a frenzy of breath
and falls in a trickle,
Then we lie exhausted in a grave, bodies
consumed yet they raise,
Time melts thawed a frosty reality to dissolve ice
without a stumble,
(You fell across this hallucinogenic Cosmos, those
stars humble).

An incarnation of Sappho and her friend
accidentally OD.

Some yell with spite and call it love, but not us, not
in a temple of Aphrodite. Here Sappho tends a
flame which brushes her lips; they are burning and
red … now purple as the heroin hit hard like a
hammer thumping its heat up the arm into the
galaxy of welcoming brain cells. The hypodermic
hangs limply from her arm, I gently draw the spike
out of the bruised vein, her arm flops diagonally
across an orange cotton shirt, I clean the syringe
by rhythmically flushing water in and out and then
Finally, squirt the crimson juice into a blue china
 Bowl: next, prepare my hit; we uncurl in a temple
Of Aphrodite, which is where lovers can purr
softly,
the floor opens like a gaping mouth and gobbles
both of us
                    UP.

The ghost of Ulrike Meinhof addresses the
bourgeoisie.
                    (Ulrike Meinhof 1934-1976.)

Our waves will wash away the sand into a sea,
Bourgeois fuckers, your system is screwed,

Ripped off the poor and the tenants,
A hot and dry summer will scorch with fire and
now burn baby burn.

Think you are stable, no just sinking into an ocean
of Narcissism which is not pretty, never learn
bourgeois,
Now your houses are being repossessed, and
those mind's twang:
those robbed of their dreams now awake;
you will be shaking in your shoes as the ghettos
buzz,
Start to tremble you have failed, and now the red
revolutionary Nemesis awaits.
The Angry Brigade is aware and alert, and the
Red Army Faction has not forgotten,
Socialist Patients Collective flex their minds, and
their trigger-fingers are twitching,
Do not think that the Red Brigades are
all banged up inside.

Our waves will wash away the sand into a sea,
Bourgeois fuckers, your system is screwed,
Ripped off the poor and the tenants,
A hot and dry summer will scorch with fire and
now burn baby burn.

They were so astonished, astounded that a
member of the intelligentsia became an
Urban guerrilla.
Ulrike, they exhumed your brain after a dreaded
death to try and solve their puzzle.

Greek partisans. [A villanelle].

The dawn awakes, we are cloaked in snow,
 Snow melts to leave bare and bleak terrain,
 My cloak is red, unlike that of a black crow.

This morning I know that knife will glow,
 I shall shake with shame, with the stain,
 The dawn awakes, we are cloaked in snow,

Some do not know the heaving lava below,
Or seasonal cruelty with that brutal blame,
My cloak is red, unlike that of a black crow.

A vocation of pain the shepherds do know,
We herd the innocents and see their pain,
The dawn awakes, we are cloaked in snow,

No, do not bow to that ancient status quo,
An act of revolt she who could never fain,
My cloak is red, unlike that of a black crow.

In Greek hills, our blood must always flow,
For Sappho, the struggle has a bloodstain,
The dawn awakes, we are cloaked in snow,
My cloak is red, unlike that of a black crow.

Lost for words with Wordsworth. Constructed from
'found' passages in William Wordsworth: Preface
to Lyrical Ballads & The Prelude.

Poetry is the spontaneous outpouring
of emotion, bliss it was to be alive yet
to be young was very heaven, when
recollected in tranquillity as a prelude.

The Sonnet was written by a latter-day Katherine
Philips (1632-1664).
        (author of Against Love).
Should I compare you to a statue of steel,
My sheep know this is a time of delusion,
        At Mass, they fear to feast upon the meal,
        We dry our sea of tears without an illusion.
        That hum of minds was like a bloody buzz,
        He was a wire on fire like a ghost on gas,
        Our school of thought was not jiving jazz,
        The man with radar that zooms into cash.
        His type is not for us because we fought,
        Remained in banks like a painted clown,
        He became green, the dollar was bought,
        The tide has turned; we gazed and frown.
        The God who reads these wise finite lines,
        I have a fear of Him for I know those signs.

Psychiatric nurses try reading some Dostoevsky.

The psychiatric nurse always wears a smile of
roses,
 But when she opens her mouth, only the thorns
show,
They rip into us like mercury is rising up a
thermometer,
But we are Mercury; we are those messengers of
words,
Communication is sanity until an abyss stare's
back at us,
Our emotional temperature is wrong, perceptions
askew,
So chant the nurses as they prostrate themselves
before

'THE SELF'
In its glory and feel one of the few, a mental health
professional,
We break the shackles on the nurse's ego and
drag them from
Their shallows of grey bourgeois murk, then, quite
the reaction,
They have a deranged duck moment of insight
here and incisive
Understanding there a magic diagnosis, nurse
read Dostoevsky,
Just step into a world of underground people as
you amuse us.

To an anonymous woman poet
met in 1941.

This woman is manna on the breeze,
And is the wind that plays my chimes,
The hands that play and stroke a harp,
You hold both an ancient quill and pen.

She welcomes with warmth, shy, sharp,
Responds with moonbeams on her lips,
But memory is like some tightened strap,
The heat of summer melts those buckles.

Fingernails dig into her temple of a body,
Mine just resembles your twisted shrine,
The tubes of lace are torn and ruptured,
It began to seep out, the yellowish fog.

We can only taste that creeping aroma,
The cyanide pellets crushed intoxicate,
She, my lunar soliloquist, has departed,
I choke on vapour, a last gasp grasped.

Commentary.
True poetry (inspired by the Muse and her prime symbol, the
moon) even today is a survival, or intuitive re-creation, of the ancient Goddess-worship.
-        Robert Graves, (1999) The White Goddess: A Historical Grammar of Poetic Myth (London, Faber & Faber p ix-x).

England has had many learned women...and yet where are the poetesses...I look everywhere for grandmothers and see none.
- Frederick G. Kenyon (1897) (ed.), The Letters of Elizabet Barrett Browning (New York, Macmillan), vol. 1. pp. 230–232.

There is an inherent tension, a dialectical contradiction, between these positions. Firstly, Graves (1999. p ix-x) argues for the supremacy of the feminine in poetry as an inherent trait. Alternatively, Elizabeth Barrett Browning (1897; vol 1 pp 230-232) suggests a lack of poetesses in print in the 1840s. How can this be explained? For my cycle's purposes, I will accept the cogency of Elizabeth Barrett Browning's position here whilst noting that it ignores women writers outside of the Canon, such as labouring class poets like Anne Yearsley and other 'hidden histories' (Wu, Duncan (1997) Romantic Women Poets: An Anthology. New Jersey, John Wiley & Sons). I concur with Graves that The Lunar Muse is the source of poetic inspiration, but women were and, to an extent, are excluded from the Canon. Those who are given preeminent status are often outsiders. Sandra Gilbert is illustrative:

Though I never met Sylvia Plath. I can honestly say that I have known her all my life.
-        Claire Brennan (2000) (ed) The Poetry of Sylvia Plath (Cambridge, Icon Books) p.52.

Therefore, my poetry will explore the nature of male poetic responses to women's poetry in patriarchal societies. Those after the creation of a 'social surplus product', the rise of class society and what Frederick Engels called 'the world-historic defeat of the female sex.' (Royle, Camilla (2020) A Rebels Guide to Engels (London, Bookmarks) p. 45.)

Sappho was, of course, known as the 'Tenth Muse' in Antiquity and consistently with my general thesis, she was much admired in that epoch. She served as a priestess of Aphrodite on the island of Lesbos. Nevertheless, as Patriarchy became further established, her poetry was demonised and even burnt on medieval popes' orders.

The first two poems are sonnets and are written with the grain of that genre; they pertain to 'romantic love'. One is to Anne Sexton (Sexton, Anne,1984 Collected Poems, Boston, Houghton Mifflin) and (Middlebrook, Diane, 1992, Anne Sexton: a biography U.S.A., Random House) provides a penetrating insight into this complex woman who like her contemporary, Sylvia Plath, would commit suicide. The next Sonnet, also, is written as a love poem to Elise Cowen, a Beat poet. See my paper: https://www.academia.edu/27823900/Elise_Cowen_poetry_on_the_margins

The only collection is Tony Trigilio ((ed) Elise Cowen: Poems and Fragments (Ahsahta Press). Elise would jump through a closed window to her death at the age of 28 in 1963; it will never be known conclusively why. Although unpublished in her lifetime, she is now regarded as a significant poet of the Beat genre. In the first English Sonnets, the 'gemell' or couplet' (Fuller (2018) p. 14) is consistent with the 'turn' and, therefore, the 'form' is emotionally heavily weighted and concludes the 'argument' satisfactorily.

The third Sonnet, which occurs towards the end of the cycle, Sonnet was written by a latter-day Katherine Philips (author of Against Love), is written from a woman's P.O.V. and against the genre while maintaining its form. This raises whether language and its formal genres are patriarchal (See Spender, Dale (1980) Man-Made Language. London, Routledge & Kegan Paul). Spender's position on Patriarchy and its accompanying linguistic systems was encapsulated here in some concluding remarks:

…the most constructive thing women can do in these circumstances is to write, for in the act of writing we deny our mutedness…
-        Spender (1980), p. 232.

The poems I am the lost child of Simone de Beauvoir, The ghost of Ulrike Meinhof addresses the bourgeoisie, and Psychiatric nurses try reading some Dostoevsky all represent a departure from the 'closed form' and are in the tradition which came to one of its moments of fruition in the poetry of Frank O'Hara mentioned in Block 3. One that can be seen as emanating from T.S. Eliot (1917), 'Vers libre is a genuine verse-form, will have a positive definition. And I can define it only in negatives: (1) absence of pattern, (2) absence of rhyme, (3) absence of metre.' http://world.std.com/~raparker/exploring/tseliot/wor ks/essays/reflections_on_vers_libre.html. Or equally, as a young Ezra Pound argued in A Retrospect (1918): "As regarding rhythm to compose in the sequence of the musical phrase, not in sequence of a metronome." (Hirsch, Edward [ed] 2014 A Poet's Glossary, New York, Houghton Mifflin Harcourt p. 244). I also was inspired, to an extent, by Blast magazine edited by

Wyndham Lewis in two editions (1914/1915) BLAST No. 1, the Vorticist magazine - The British Library https://www.bl.uk/collection-items/blast-no-1-the-vorticist. Hence my use of typeset: 'THE SELF' in the poem Psychiatric Nurses try reading some Dostoevsky. Although both Pound and Wyndham Lewis would develop abhorrent pro-fascist/Hitlerite beliefs in the 1930s. The ghost of Ulrike Meinhof addresses the bourgeoisie's finds an intertextual origin in Diane di Prima (2007) Revolutionary Letters (San Francisco, Last Gasp of San Francisco). I employ idiolect in this poem. There is a general appreciation of the poetry of Vladimir Mayakovsky, who shot himself rather than betray the October 1917 revolution and become a mouthpiece for the counter-revolution and Stalin, see (Carrick, Rosy (2015) [ed], Volodya: Mayakovsky Selected Works (London, Enitharmon Press).

My development as a writer during A802 has been characterised by several elements. Firstly, a concretisation of my poetry. This was achieved by adjusting my use of imagery, simile, and metaphor with my tutor's guidance through T.M.A. feedback and telephone/online tutorials. The observations of other students about P.O.V. were also valuable, particularly in the module's early stages. I have learnt to adjust metre in accordance with the poet's meaning as the course continued. The cross-fertilisation with prose was helpful because a prose narrative opened up dimensions of 'time' and reinforced structural considerations. I would maintain that these gains have made my poetry more accessible. Ultimately, I utilise both Modernist and New Formalist techniques. Although I have some sympathy with Samuel Taylor Coleridge's comment: 'I write in metre because I am about to use a language different to prose.' However, finally, for the poet who wishes to challenge Patriarchy, she or he would do well to write like Sylvia Plath: 'The blood jet is poetry/There is no stopping it.' (Plath, Sylvia (1981) Sylvia Plath Collected Poems, London, Faber and Faber, p.270).

Bibliography.

Addonizio, Kim, & Laux, Dorianne (1997) The Poet's Companion: A Guide to the Pleasures of Writing Poetry. (Norton & Company, London).

BLAST No. 1, (1914) the Vorticist magazine - The British Library https://www.bl.uk/collection-items/blast-no-1-the-vorticist.

Brennan, Claire (2000) [ed] The Poetry of Sylvia Plath (Cambridge, Icon Books).

Browning, Barret Elizabeth (1995) Aurora Leigh and Other Poems, (London, Penguin Classics).

Carrick, Rosy (2015) [ed], Volodya: Mayakovsky Selected Works (London, Enitharmon Press).

Coleridge, Samuel-Taylor (2008) Samuel Taylor Coleridge, The Major Works (Oxford, Oxford World's Classics)

de Beauvoir, Simone (2009) The Second Sex. Trans. Constance Borde and Sheila Malovany-Chevallier. (Random House: Alfred A. Knopf).

Di Prima, Diane (2007) Revolutionary Letters (San Francisco, Last Gasp of San Francisco).

Dostoyevsky, Fyodor (2011) Notes from Underground (New York, Vintage Classics).

Duffy, Carol Ann (2015) Collected Poems (London, Picador).

Eliot, T.S. (1917) Reflections on Vers Libre http://world.std.com/~raparker/exploring/tseliot/works/essays/reflections_on_vers_libre.html

Engels, Frederick (2010) The Origin of the Family, Private Property, and the State (London, Penguin Classics).

Finch, Annie (2009) A Poet's Craft: The Making and Shaping of Poems (U.S.A., University of Michigan Press.)

Foley, Barbara (2019) Marxist Literary Criticism Today (London, Pluto Press).

Frederick G. Kenyon (1897) (ed.), The Letters of Elizabeth Barrett Browning (New York, Macmillan), vol. 1.

Frost, Robert (2001) The Collected Poems (London, Vintage Classics).

Fuller, John (2018) The Sonnet: The Critical Idiom Reissued, (London, Routledge).

Graves, Robert (2003) The Complete Poems (London, Penguin Classics).

Graves, Robert (1999) The White Goddess: A Historical Grammar of Poetic Myth (London, Faber & Faber).

Häublein, Ernst (2018) The Stanza: The Critical Idiom Reissued, (London, Routledge.)

Hollander, John (1981) Rhyme's Reason. (London, Yale University Press.)

Hirsch, Edward [ed] 2014 A Poet's Glossary, (New York, Houghton Mifflin Harcourt.)

Iain, Gill & Sellers, Susan (2007) A History of Feminist Literary Criticism, (Cambridge, Cambridge University Press.)

Lockward, Diane, (2018) The Practicing Poet: Writing Beyond the Basics (New Jersey, Terrapin Books)

Lucie-Smith, Edward (1979) [ed] British Poetry since 1945 (Harmondsworth, Penguin Books.)

Marx, Eleanor & Aveling, Edward (1886) The Women Question from a Socialist Point of View. https://www.marxists.org › archive › eleanor-marx › works › woman

Marx & Engels (1973) On Literature and Art. A Selection of Writings, [eds] L. Baxandall and S. Mora (St. Louis, Milwaukee).

Middlebrook, Diane, (1992), Anne Sexton: a biography (U.S.A, Random House).

Millett, Kate (2000) Sexual Politics, (Urbana and Chicago, University of Illinois Press).

O'Hara, Frank (2005) Selected Poems. (Manchester, Carcanet Press Ltd).

Orr, Judith (2015) Marxism and Women's Liberation. (London, Bookmarks).

Patterson, Don (2015) 40 Sonnets. (London, Faber & Faber).

Pearce, Nigel. Elise Cowen: Poetry on the margins.
https://www.academia.edu/27823900/Elise_Cowen_poetry_on_the_margins

Plath, Sylvia (1981) Sylvia Plath Collected Poems, (London, Faber & Faber).

Philips, Katherine Against Love
https://en.wikisource.org/wiki/Against_Love_(Philips)

Pound, Ezra (1948) [intro: T.S. Eliot] Selected Poems (London Faber & Faber).

Rosenberg, Chanie (1998) (ed) Alexandra Kollontai on Women's Liberation (London, Bookmarks).

Royle, Camilla (2020) A Rebels Guide to Engels (London, Bookmarks).

Sappho
https://www.poetryfoundation.org/poets/sappho

Sexton, Anne, (1984) Collected Poems, (Boston, Houghton Mifflin.)

Showalter, Elaine (2009) A Literature of Their Own: British Women Novelists from Brontë to Lessing. (London, Virago, Revised Edition).

Spender, Dale (1980) Man-Made Language. (London, Routledge & Kegan Paul).

Trigilio, Tony (2014). (ed) Elise Cowen: Poems and Fragments, Ahsahta Press.

Waldron, Mary (1996) Luctilla, Milkmaid of Clifton: The Life and Writings of Anne Yearsley, 1753-1806.

Wordsworth, William (2008) The Complete Works (Oxford, Oxford World Classics).

Wu, Duncan (1997) [ed] Romantic Women Poets: An Anthology. (New Jersey, John Wiley & Sons).

Our Lady of Sorrows in Notting Hill Gate (1973)

That green-scaled goddess of grief how she is wailing from her brown soil grave,
It is here that the recently resurrected dead exchange their laughter without any lament,
But you, who are skeletal with yellow skin pulled tight in a smile of delight, you,
A beatified Courtesan who roams these connected on electrified tuned-in grids,
A heart wrapped in sackcloth, which is worn by those incipient lovers of chaos,
Here a frozen embryo begins to pulsate, it breaths with the bitter pulp of those apples bit in the Garden of Pleasure,

Ice folds into our eyes until lost we are reborn into
this spectrum of zoned silence,
I embrace you; you took the crucifixion from my
eyes, and our eyes do bleed bliss.

Morpheus and William Burroughs (a
Petrarchan sonnet.)

We groove along furrows to cut the wet pavement,
This street reflects an inner web, this glassy maze,
The path to oblivion, it melts like an echo of
praise,
The temple begins to sing with an awaking
ferment,
The dream-powder, its magic is like night's scent,
A garden of delight where sight and tears are
glazed.
You spike the mainline again; this is not so
crazed,
 The cobweb is caught like a dream's finite
content.

But Morpheus is a cruel god, in darkness confess,
His bonds, we know his mellow, like a nocturne,
 We were naked, our mind's flow does dissolve,
 A cloud whose rain which beats us nails, Venus
Always burns away my colours in eyes not
taciturn,
 What remains, the riddles of thought, always
turn?

A beat moment in a Beat life: A dramatic
monologue.

Those square hearts had stopped,
they were
Just rusty bilge pumps,
someone had turned
Their switch off, what a turn-on
We never dug that scene with America,
The atom bombs, we chant with those
Of us who had a different sound
and song
to the hooded-snake death dirge, breathe the
snow
wind of pure purgation, howl cathartic
baby burnout
buzz
madness.
William placed enigma in caps, opened that cap,
cooked it, fixed it, again, hazy.
DECONDITIONED OURSELVES FROM STATE
SUBLIMINAL MANIPULATION,
Bill had a sweet-death golden flight of Icarus, that
perpetual labour of Sisyphus,
I missed your tube shit there goes a decent rush,
blood looks very dark, hepatitis?

Unlike us, Allen, some did get clean, but their
purple lights remain floating free.

Speaking of viral poetry: a prose poem.

Language is a virus from outer space...The author is simply a node on a network, through which ideas pass.

- William Burroughs, The Ticket that Exploded, 1962.

That fatigue can no longer frighten us like the ice sheets in mind, it is beyond any vestige or manifestation of fear as glaring of sun drills eyes. The black petals begin to fold inwards when a gaze is or isn't fixed, tangles of twisted thorns of a tight thistle bush are forests of emptiness, viral poetry is written and formed into lakes of ice, from ice is refined the pure crystals that are polished into those old cold stars, they had imploded long ago creating the gulping black holes. Babies' mouths who drink from a nipple which oozes dark milk, it's ancient not nectar, it is the ingestion of the 'Other', us as a dark subject, objectification is unmade. Promenaded people wake up and do not think black holes are empty, scabby fingers are grasping the bourgeois hand that shivers with revulsion, grey-suited exorcists wail 'demon get out', but we existed for aeons before Eden or logos; our word is an infectious virus. For you are totally helpless, we have convinced your best philosophers since Epicurus and inspired the poet Sappho, then lit the fuse around October 1917. We are the Virus made word, made material in your universe because our cells have penetrated it.

A poem for William Burroughs.
I saw the best minds of my generation destroyed
by madness, starving hysterical naked, dragging
themselves through the streets at dawn looking for
a fix.

- Allen Ginsberg, Howl, 1956.

Staring streets reflect the voids in your eyes
which are mirrors of the squares,
They exist without the pricking needle easing
chaos; you found the mainline again,
An embrace like an orgasm burning through a
vein, Zen with and without the hassle,
This Light strikes those chemical cells calling
calmly to the soul like that whispered
welcome of nothingness,
The Absurdity is not in these oceans where
weeping tranquillity tumbles into dreams for you
were dancing into the masquerades of non-being.
High womb-like peace sleep, wake, write, weep,
fix again. You survived, died at 83 because being
you, you always 'went first'.

Summer of love, 1967. (a villanelle).

Time melts: we thawed a frosty reality to dissolve
ice with our love,
Our eyes whose dilated pupils could swallow any
hardened gaze,
(You fell across this hallucinogenic Cosmos, these
stars tumble).

We crucified the betrayal of damned love and
stared to humble.
 That dark spark, we conceived this just like
evaporating into a haze,
 Time melts: we thawed a frosty reality to dissolve
ice with our love,

 I touched with delicate fingers the clasp on your
eyes to unbuckle.
A stream, the purple fragrance of humming, a
goddess was ablaze,
 (You fell across this hallucinogenic Cosmos,
these stars tumble).

You crumpled into a sphere of sighs encircled by
white Light, a dove,
 Whose wings were caressed as we dived into the
sun in a daze,
Time melts: we thawed a frosty reality to dissolve
ice with our love.

Our song was vibrating into weeping trees, nectar
dripping, suckle,
 The other's ancient milk, which is a sacred
libation with soft praise,

(You fell across this hallucinogenic Cosmos, these stars tumble).

Tangerine gasp intertwines in a frenzy of breath, it falls from above,
Then we lie exhausted in a grave, our bodies consumed, but raised,
Time melts: we thawed a frosty reality to dissolve ice with our love.

Prose-poem to 'tribunes of the oppressed' when 'clean'.
Man was born free, and he is everywhere in chains. Those who think themselves the masters of others are indeed greater slaves than they.
— Jean-Jacques Rousseau, The Social Contract, 1762.

The moon rises like mist distilled from a burnt river to whirl with her humming until the bonds unravel. Now she is caressing her smile into the radiant morning; her dust is lingering it sprinkles onto dormant souls of night awaking our song of love to a golden dawn. The poet's pen is dipping into this chalice of Light we wander across pages with infinity and innocence. Dance with the Light and shadows of the sacred ritual, this is a Psalm of joy to a pristine moon and drowsy sun, you and I, humanity.

Yet she and he know the multitudes remain in shackles, some of iron, steel, or gold. Not until we

'tribunes of the oppressed' have severed, sawn
every fetter can we rest.

Haiku.
A pillar of stone
Has a cloak of golden light.
It wraps itself in.

Haiku on poets.
Cut our mind of coils
 And it bleeds an ink of joy.
That stain lemon stars.

Commentary.
These poems were initially derived from my
reading of Horovitz, M. (1969) Children of Albion,
Poetry of the Underground in Britain, London,
Penguin Books. Also influential were collections of
American underground writing including Allen
Ginsburg's work, William S. Burroughs'
experimental prose, the poetry of Diane De Prima
& Elise Cowen as well as Frank O'Hara and The
New York School.

Again, for Sylvia Plath.

I am in your repose rested in a speckled rose
grave,
    A tomb in a canopy of willows weeping,
Your bejewelled soul is purple and enticing my
fountain pen weaves willow within it.

An entombed fragrance can be so sweetly stoned,
    Ablaze with your lights legal and purple,
My pen murmured and ejaculated on a page
      'poetry is the blood jet.'
      You said.

    An Elegy for Graham upon pondering
W. H. Auden
      Musee des Beaux-Arts, 1938.

Ablaze this Icarus fell from the ticked time,
Auden missed the point in that 1938 rhyme,
I heard your voice aloud in the baying pack
Of mental nurses, they walk with a whack.

A cut of words was sharp and yelled aloud,
You spoke with Laing and chanted so proud,
We told of a world of flowers and revolution,
The staff still smear us; they have no solution.

Phone erupted, and anonymity croaked death,
A slip of the tongue, just Freudian foul breath,
Could be a trap set by those greened eyed,

My abbey echoed with words sighs it cried.

And death has dominion; it drinks with a thirst,
That silver chalice has wine which is our dust.

Another Adonis.

Looked into your eyes and saw a galaxy of stars,
They glared like an untameable beam of death,
Like your beloved Lennard Cohen words were
Almost like syllables roughed, coughed, howled,
A cheetah glanced out of the shadow but always
Would purr in imperfect pulses in that asymmetry,
But whoever wanted to be a square like a sheep?

There was a disequilibrium in your pure metre,
Always the day dawned and danced its words,
We waltzed our minds into a cloud of unknowing.

The scroll did not roll out for the staid sane pens,
Our pens etched souls of amber wrote the words
That reverberated like loss and love petrification,
We made pyres of words, tried to purge the pain.

A Tiger.

A tiger burnt cold as he circled a herd of zebra,
I await his next stitch as there is always a needle,
It starts with moves and little drinky poos for free,
But nothing is free with him, too long behind bars

Of pubs and prisons, a peppermint crème oozes,
Now he has charmed again 'have these Blues,'
His insurance policy whirled into one more oasis,
Why does he decide to deceive the stripy flocks?

Because he has nothing to fool within but a void,
Avoid I would if it were at all possible as it bores,
What of 'tribunes of the oppressed' if not when?
But herds of zebra are dispensable as not lions.

I guess a 'crash-pad' is better than the streets,
Shame about the zebra though.

But do you not blink at their gangrene gouged
Limbs,
Those ordered lines of stigmata upon stigmata,

It all started with little drinky poos.

He remembered Elise Cowen and
glanced three times at a lightbulb.

(A prose-poem.)

He sits in a sea of yellow custard cushions
observing a solitary lightbulb. It is suspended,
dangles like his mind, by a single withered cord. It
is pulsating slightly, or so it seems; no, it is the
bulb flickering. The room is like a cube of pure
white, but fingers of red light and shadow caress
it. The darkness is merging into the dawn. The
rays of light and electricity compete lazily. The
daybreak is peeping through threadbare green
curtains which do hang across greyish plastic-
coated steel wires suspended between two
bronzed hooks, the Alpha and the Omega, the
Word and the deed which must follow. He squints
around and finds his feet and glides around to
discover a stained square of plastic, here is the
switch, he clicks it off, the bulb extinguished, and
so did his mind. He plunged into an ocean of
crawling patterns that dissolve like mirrors of soft
wax. Then located the switch, pushed the
rectangle within what has become an oblong, but
dawn awaits outside in the world.

In that place lurk purple serpents with green eyes
composed of composite deceptions, ice that burns
like Sulphur of hell. I had fled, knowing I am both
ice and purgatory. My heart is both torn and
crimson, yet it is not cold or black nor twisted but
beats blood. I pick up a knife to defend myself
from the serpents but then realise I had not slept

for many days and nights. There is no glint from the blade because the moon had imploded. Where is everyone? Noting dark red stains on my clothes, I just plunged the knife inwards. A siren as if from Ulysses' longest sentence tied ribbons of words around my body. Yes, it was Joyce and the twisted and winding sentence written in 1922, which had held 3,687 words. Cast upon rocks and wrecked yet bound with a tape measure of black and white, comments on cotton, ideas in heads, Beauty is Truth and that is all I need to know on Earth spoken by John Keats.

.

Now I was happy to sleep.

On 'Spooks.'
A Petrarchan Sonnet.

You speak in heighten phraseology,
You had believed our fight soulless,
But never had avoided us on purpose,
A tape records a list of pharmacology.
We chat using only Leftist terminology,
We talk in words that are meaningless,
We wink again as they are senseless,
And then grimace at their eschatology.

Our Nemesis will tear down their dawn,
They are already marked in pens of red,
Then crawl into rabbit holes hidden down,
But will only bury those they put into bed,
Were lobotomised when in Portland Down,
Those zombies had served the living dead.

Two traditional Haiku.

01.

Summer has fragrant
Love with sweet scent, in moonlight
We can only weep.

02.

Cherry blossom crowns
The lovers' summer, madman
Your blossom is hail.

A modern Haiku.

A haiku written in memory of Edie Sedgwick (1943-1971).

Bliss was fixing fire
In shadows, flower of flame
You wilted to bloom.

Commentary.

Spectres overshadow these poems. Sylvia Plath is preeminent in this sequence because she encapsulates the enigma of my writing (Plath, 1986, p.35):

Why do I spend my life writing?

[…]
I write only because
There is a voice within me
That will not be still.

She was such an innovator and challenged the Patriarchal discourse. She also created with Robert Lowell, and Anne Sexton a new genre, Confessional Writing. This does not mean that my work is simply 'confessional.' Because for the writer, I argue, after the debates on authorial intent around the 'Intentional Fallacy' developed by W. K. Wimsatt & Monroe C. Beardsley in 1948 (The Verbal Icon 1954). The goal of poetry is not merely the reproduction of the 'self'. Indeed, Emily Dickinson is an excellent example of the poet who manifests a diversity of poetic persona.

However, is poetry a Platonic 'form' which is 'outside' of History? Trotsky provided a sophisticated analysis (Leon Trotsky: Class and Art (1924) - Marxists Internet Archive):

> Dante was, of course, the product of a certain social milieu. But Dante was a genius. He raised the experience of his epoch to a tremendous artistic height.

We have a model which is dialectical and transcends Stalinist 'vulgar Marxism.'

Although I employ both isometric and heterometric stanzaic patterns, my sequence begins with an Ars Poetica piece synthesising my writing with my Muse. I decided to start vers libre, acknowledging Modernism and Plath's role in the genre. I quote her. The next poem is an elegy in response to a recent death. After posting it on the Forum, I made P.O.V. alterations. Also, challenged Dylan Thomas booming line by stating 'death has dominion'. I referenced a hollow Requiem Mass with a final heroic couplet which has masculine rhymes on conclusive consonants 'st, st'. Another Adonis employs alliteration, hammering the pain into a reader who might not have experienced a string of suicides in the final stanza —especially' S' and 'P' letters. A Tiger is a short free-verse narrative poem about a calculating person who ensnared the vulnerable. The metaphors employed here are a tiger and zebra, both striped but opposites. I 'show' possible consequences with 'gangrene gouged limbs' where needle marks 'ordered lines of stigmata upon stigmata'. A refusal of the Left quoting Lenin 'tribunes of the oppressed' to assist. It concludes consistently with its 'form' in a moral. However, its language is 'multi-accentual' and has something of an 'inner dialectic quality.' (Volosinov,1996 p, 23). A prose-poem was an appropriate vehicle for a hallucinogenic experience alluding to Elise Cowen's short life [she jumped through a closed window to her death after her parents discharged her from psychiatric hospital]. She was 'close' to Allen Ginsburg who would only refer to her as 'the intellectual madwoman' in the aftermath. In a Petrarchan Sonnet, I write against the genre to describe the 'secret police'. Therefore, reflecting the predicament, some British writers experienced in the context of imperialism in their backyard, Ireland (Wheatly, 2015 p. 56-59). The volta answers the problem posed as the sonnet picks up pace (See Fussell, 1979, pp 115-116).

Finally, I wrote in another traditional form, Haiku. Although only relatively recently imported into the West and conclude with a framing haiku with Edie Sedgwick's premature death mirroring Sylvia Plath's at the beginning of the sequence.

Bibliography.

Alvarez, A. (1974) The Savage God: A Study of Suicide, Harmondsworth, Penguin Books.

Barnard College (alumnae Elise Cowen). https://barnardarchives.wordpress.com/2002/08/13/elise-nada-cowen-56/

Caldwell, A & Hardwick, O. (2019) [ed] The Valley Anthology of Prose Poetry, Scarborough, Valley Press.

Frost, R (2013) The Collected Poems, London, Vintage.

Fussell, P (1979), Poetic Meter and Poetic Form, revised edition, New York, McGraw-Hill, Inc.

Hirsch, E (1999) How to Read a Poem and Fall in Love with Poetry, Boston, Mariner Books.

Lenin, V.I. (1901/1902) What Is to Be Done? https://www.marxists.org/archive/lenin/works/1901/witbd/

McDowell, G.L & Rzicznek, D, F (2010) Field Guide to Prose Poetry: Contemporary Poets in Discussion and Practice, Massachusetts, Brookline.

Noel-Tod, J (2018) [ed]The Penguin Book of The Prose Poem, London, Penguin Classics.

Oliver, M (1994) A Poetry Handbook, Boston, Mariner Books.

Paz, O. (1986). The Poems of Octavio Paz, New York, New Directions Books.

Pearce, N. (2008) Elise Cowen: Poetry on the Margins: https://www.academia.edu/27823900/Elise_Cowen_poetry_on_the_margins

Plath, S (1983) Collected Poems, London, Faber & Faber.

Plath, S (1986) [ed]. Plath, A.S, Sylvia Plath, Letters Home: Correspondence 1950-1963, London, Faber & Faber.

Samson, P (2013) Writing Poems, Northumberland, Broadaxe Books.

Stand, M & Boland, E (2001) [ed] The Making of a Poem, London, W.W. Norton & Company.

Stevens, W (1923) Of Modern Poetry, https://www.poetryfoundation.org/poems/43435/of-modern-poetry

Stevens, W (2010) Selected Poems, London, Faber & Faber.

Thomas, D (2016) The Collected Poems of Dylan Thomas: The Centenary Edition, London, Weidenfeld & Nicolson.

Trotsky, L. (1924) Class and Art, Leon Trotsky: Class and Art (1924) - Marxists Internet Archive

Volosinov, V.N. ([1929] 1996) Marxism and the Philosophy of Language, Massachusetts, Harvard University Press.

Wheatly, D (2015) Contemporary British Poetry, London, Palgrave.

Williams, R (2013) The Poetry Toolkit: the essential guide to studying poetry, 2nd Edition, London, Bloomsbury.

Wimsatt, W. K. (1954) The Verbal Icon, Kentucky, University of Kentucky Press.

Yeats, W. B. (1992), [ed]. Albright, D W. B. Yeats, The Poems, London,

(Lines upon reading Charlotte Mew:
'Magdeleine in Church'*).
Our breath heavy, honeyed, tortured, and curved,
Shiny black boots were dark and gloss orbit in sin,
      She was almost a stormtrooper when
enraptured,
      I rolled into a ball and hoped not to sing
that hymn.
That whip was raised as if on 1936 Olympian day,
It cracked with whacks like goose-stepping troops,
      Can they love like sheep who come on
Sunday?
You and I, we know the meaning of our troupes.
Is sin delight Mary when Our Lady was so far
      Away, only had drunk with sad and evil
men,
So had laid in a gutter while we gazed at a star,
Then crawled to Mass, read Nietzsche a madman.
If God was dead, all that remains is absurd
vocation,
For that ball and chain never gave her satisfaction.

*Charlotte Mew's poem, the longest she wrote @
222 lines, Magdeleine in Church. The first printers
refused to set it when published in her debut
collection, The Farmer's Bride (1916). Julia Copus
(2021), in her biography, provides two possible
reasons. First, the printers may have been
genuinely outraged on religious grounds or, more
likely, because DH Lawrence's The Rainbow had
been banned and publicly burned recently, they
were frightened.

The Steppenwolf.

A wolf had wandered the Steppes in a dance of
solitude;
that desert of snow had stretched endlessly; it
glistened,
Those expanses had no horizon; rays burned his
eyes
And burrowed into a heart woven of silk, this is the
price
He paid for his emancipation, an escape into a
wasteland.

Tracks left will soon melt, for he leaves no mark,
The only mark is the one that cuts into his heart,
 From which he knows there can be no escape.

Frosted wastelands seemed today both caustic
and angry;
 that sanctuary has imploded into icicles that cut,
little mercy,
The Steppenwolf sniffed the air; it was chill like the
slap of cold,
Then sets steady yellow eyes on the precipice and
hurls himself.

A shepherd who carried a shaft of poetry secured
by goat skin,
He wandered across a fertile valley with the tribe it
was a flock,
So stumbled upon the corpse of the Steppenwolf,
man or wolf,
Then rummaged through belongings to find a wad
of poems.

To transcribe these documents for three days and
nights,
The Steppenwolf was resurrected and then had a
tomb,
  Comprised of words, scrawled notes, and
manuscripts.

CPSIA information can be obtained
at www.ICGtesting.com
Printed in the USA
LVHW042101150922
728494LV00004B/66

9 781783 826414